Shakespeare

in the Stratford Records

ROBERT BEARMAN

THE SHAKESPEARE BIRTHPLACE TRUST
ALAN SUTTON PUBLISHING LTD.

First published in the United Kingdom in 1994
Alan Sutton Publishing Ltd · Phoenix Mill · Far Thrupp · Stroud
Gloucestershire

First published in the United States of America in 1994
Alan Sutton Publishing Inc · 83 Washington Street · Dover
NH 03820

Published in association with the Shakespeare Birthplace Trust
The Shakespeare Centre · Henley Street · Stratford-upon-Avon

British Library Cataloguing in Publication Data

A catalogue record for this book is available from the British Library.

Library of Congress Cataloging in Publication Data applied for

ISBN 0–7509–0632–45

Typeset in 11/13 Bembo.
Typesetting and origination by
Alan Sutton Publishing Limited.
Printed in Great Britain by
Redwood Books, Trowbridge, Wiltshire

Contents

General Editors' Preface

The objects of the Shakespeare Birthplace Trust, as defined by the Act of Parliament under which it operates, are:

a) to promote in every part of the world the appreciation and study of the plays and other works of William Shakespeare and the general advancement of Shakespearian knowledge;
b) to maintain and preserve the Shakespeare birthplace properties for the benefit of the nation;
c) to provide and maintain for the benefit of the nation a museum and a library of books, manuscripts, records of historic interest, pictures, photographs and objects of antiquity with particular but not exclusive reference to William Shakespeare, his life, works and times.

It is from these objectives that the series of publications, of which this volume is part, derives. The central focus of the series is Shakespeare: his plays and their performance, his life, and the environment, historical, topographical, and domestic, in which he lived; and the raw material for volumes in the series is derived largely from the rich Shakespearian holdings of the Trust's Library and Records Office, in the form of printed books and archival and pictorial material relating to Shakespeare's life in Stratford, to the history of the town, to scholarship and criticism on his writings, and to the performance history of his plays. Such a collection of volumes, covering a wide range of topics – theatrical, literary and historical – cannot, of course, observe rigid editorial uniformity. To a considerable extent, therefore, treatment and approach from volume to volume are determined by the aims and needs of individual authors and editors. Within this rather broad scope, however, we seek to produce a series of volumes that will be of interest to the general reader while maintaining a high standard of scholarship in the furtherance of that basic objective of the Shakespeare Birthplace Trust, 'the general advancement of Shakespearian knowledge'.

Robert Bearman
Robert Smallwood

Preface

So many scholars have pored over the few surviving documents recording Shakespeare's life that, when I first began this study, I did not think there could be anything new to say. Indeed, so much has been written about Shakespeare that it would be a brave person to declare that he or she had succeeded in so doing. Nevertheless, it soon became clear to me that I was approaching by a different route. I had not come to my subject via academic study of Shakespeare's writings. My professional obsession is the nature of historic evidence, not Shakespeare and the Elizabethan theatre or the techniques of literary criticism. As a result, I have ventured to lay claim to one or two new observations.

Some of these are of a general nature, arising out of recent demographic and social history research, but I was also surprised to find that the documents themselves could be made to yield a little more. I have also been fortunate enough to have been able to make reference to two documents, recently discovered by Jeanne Jones and Mairi Macdonald: though not quite contemporary with Shakespeare, both throw important new light on the history of his property.

Many people have read drafts of this study and all made helpful suggestions. In this respect I am particularly indebted to Dr Robert Smallwood, Professor Stanley Wells, Dr Alan Dyer, Dr Susan Brock, Roger Pringle, Mairi Macdonald and Jeanne Jones. My sternest but most valued critic is my wife, Jan Bunyan. Nevertheless, all errors remain my own responsibility.

Robert Bearman

Introduction

There are fewer than eighty hand-written documents dating from Shakespeare's lifetime that contain a mention of his name. Other material has survived, of course, that throws light on his life without actually mentioning him; documents, for instance, relating to members of his immediate family; those entries in the Stationers' Registers that record the publication of his plays, while not naming him as the author; and documents associated with the family's application for a coat of arms, which, though almost certainly instigated by Shakespeare himself, name only his father. Other sources for his life are printed, not least the title pages of some early editions of his plays. Others again, such as Stratford's parish register, contain more than one mention of him over a period of time. Nevertheless it remains the case that during his lifetime William Shakespeare is only mentioned by name in seventy-nine hand-written documents.

None of these documents has remained precisely in the same place over the four centuries since it was written. Some, though, have had a more adventurous history than others. Shakespeare's dealings, for instance, with the Southwark tax collectors have always been part of the Public Records, continuously housed in London although in a succession of different places. Similarly, records of some of his dealings with the civic authorities in his native town have always been part of the Stratford-upon-Avon borough records. But as Shakespeare's reputation grew, scholars began to dig into these and other likely accumulations, unearthing one by one records of the dramatist's life. In the process some strayed out of the collections of which for centuries they had been part, four of them ending up abroad, in the Folger Shakespeare Library in Washington DC. Others have been gathered in again to rest alongside the collections to which they once belonged.

At present, two institutions share most of the responsibility for safeguarding these precious records. One is the Public Record Office in London, with thirty-five in its care.[1] The other is the Shakespeare Birthplace Trust in Stratford-upon-Avon, with thirty (or thirty-one if we include an ambiguous candidate). No other institution has more than four.

This publication takes a close look at those records of Shakespeare's life preserved in his native town of Stratford-upon-Avon: how they have come to be there; what their place is in the collections of records of which they are (or were) a part; and what they tell us of the dramatist's life.

CHAPTER ONE

Baptisms and Burials: the Parish Register

The first document we must consider is the earliest of Stratford-upon-Avon's parish registers, containing, among many hundreds of entries, five mentions of Shakespeare's name. These record his baptism, on 26 April 1564, the baptism of his children, Susanna, on 26 May 1583, and the twins, Hamnet and Judith, on 2 February 1585, Hamnet's burial on 11 August 1596 and his own burial on 25 April 1616.[1]

The register in which these entries occur measures 17½ × 7½ × 3 inches and, despite several rebindings, retains its brown leather cover, brass corner-pieces ornamented with the Tudor Rose and the remains of two brass clips (p. 2). It bears the date 1600, probably the date it was purchased by the parish authorities as a result of new regulations introduced in 1598. Parish registers were supposed to have been kept since 1538, but many of them were made of paper and not well looked after. In 1598 it was decided, therefore, that these early registers should be replaced by more durable parchment ones, into which all the entries since at least the beginning of Queen Elizabeth's reign (1558) should first be copied. Once this transcribing had been done it was usual for the original to be thrown away. This is what happened in Stratford. The neat hand of the copyist ends on 15 September 1600, when the job of entering baptism, marriage and burial details was taken over by the current parish officials. The old register was then

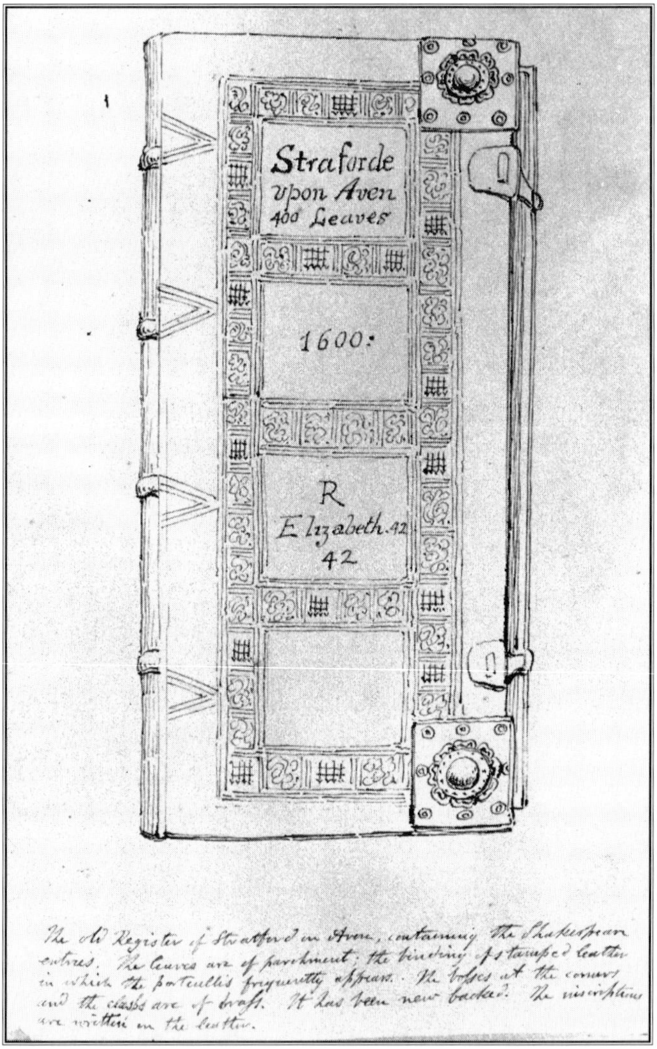

Frederick Fairholt's mid-nineteenth-century drawing and description of the Stratford parish register. The date 1600 denotes when it was acquired and when the entries from the original register (from 1558) were copied into it. (SBT, ER 1/111, f. 100)

discarded. The entries before this date, including the baptism of Shakespeare and of his children, and the burial of his son Hamnet, are therefore not the day-to-day entries made by the parish priest but part of a transcript of 1600 made by a paid copyist (pp. 4–5).

Nor is this the end of the story. The entries in the original paper registers were not made day by day: the 1538 regulations required only that they should be written up once a week, and even this was doubtless not always observed. Clearly, then, the registers in existence today could contain errors that had crept in at more than one stage of this copying and recopying. Be that as it may, the sober-minded historian, after studying the register as a whole, can only conclude that generally its entries are reliable. First children regularly occur born to fathers whose marriages can be traced within the previous twelve months; many of these children reappear shortly afterwards as infant burials; further children are born to the same fathers at a fairly regular rate of one every one to two years; widows and widowers can be found remarrying fairly soon after the burials of their former spouses, and so on. On balance, therefore, we cannot seriously doubt that William son of John Shakespeare was indeed baptized on 26 April 1564.

On what day he was born, however, is a matter for speculation. The 1559 Prayer Book instructed parents not to delay the baptism of their child at the most beyond the Sunday following birth. In 1564 26 April fell on a Wednesday, implying that, if Shakespeare's parents observed the Prayer Book's exhortation, he is unlikely to have been born earlier than Sunday 23 April. That this date coincides with the feast day of St George, the patron saint of England, has proved irresistible, and Shakespeare's birthday has come to be traditionally observed on that day.

The baptism of Shakespeare's children, Susanna in May 1583 and the twins, Hamnet and Judith, in February 1585, are likewise

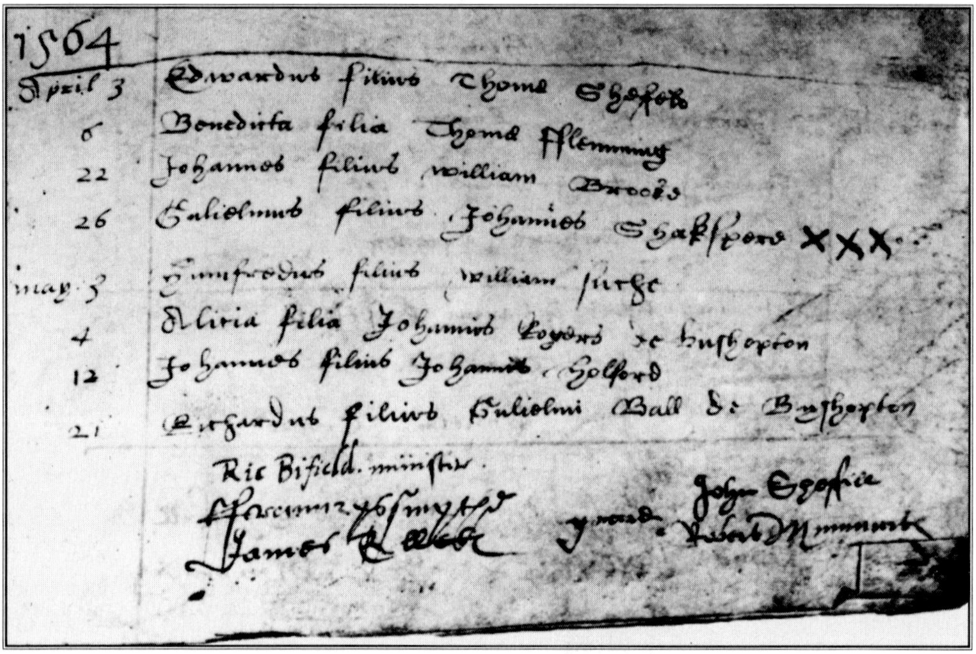

Page from the Stratford parish register recording Shakespeare's baptism; 26 April 1564. The uniform hand is that of the 1600 copyist. The certifying signatures at the bottom of the page, also dating from the time of the copy, are those of the vicar and churchwardens. (SBT, DR 243/1, baptisms, f. 5)

included in the 1600 transcript of the original paper register. Hamnet and Judith, though baptized on the same day, are not actually described in the register as twins (only as 'sonne and daughter to William Shaksper') and at a later period there are known instances of successive children of the same marriage being baptized together. However, the twenty-month interval between Susanna's baptism and Judith and Hamnet's is less than the average gap between children at that time and is certainly not long

May 6 Hugh sonne to Humphrey Holder
8 David sonne to Anthony Cooke
22 ~~Anne daughter to James Wodward~~
26 Susanna daughter to William Shakspere X
31 William sonne to John Rogers
31 Jone daughter to James Taylor

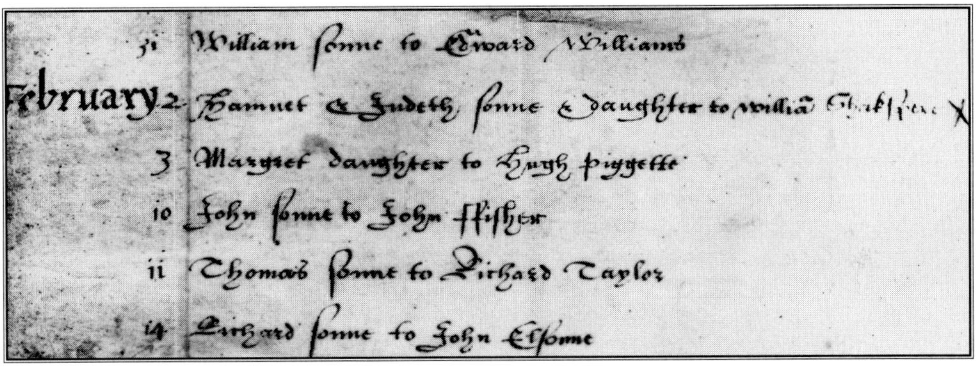
31 William sonne to Edward Williams
February 2 Hamnet & Judeth sonne & daughter to Williã Shakspere X
3 Margret daughter to Hugh Piggette
10 John sonne to John ffisher
11 Thomas sonne to Richard Taylor
14 Richard sonne to John Elsome

Entries in the Stratford parish register recording the baptisms of Shakespeare's children, Susanna (above) on 26 May 1583, and the twins, Hamnet and Judith (below), on 2 February 1585. The hand is again that of the 1600 copyist. (SBT, DR 243/1, baptisms, ff. 20v, 22v)

enough to cast any real doubt on the generally held belief that Hamnet and Judith really were twins. Nor is there any real significance in the register's failure to describe them as such. From 1561 to 1575 the Latin word *gemelli* ('twins') was used in the Stratford register almost without exception to describe pairs of children born to the same father and baptized on the same day. But from 1576 until the end of the century the opposite is the case, with the word 'twins' occurring only twice out of a possible nineteen cases. This phenomenon must surely be ascribed to a change of practice, perhaps on the appointment of a new parish clerk.

Of more interest is Susanna's baptism only six months after her parents' wedding. This by itself would not be worthy of special comment, as it has been calculated that across the country during this period at least a fifth of brides were pregnant before their marriage, although there were many local variations.[2] Indeed, in the year of Shakespeare's marriage (1582) five of the women married in Stratford's parish church had produced children within nine months of the ceremony. In contrast, for the same year, only nine children are recorded born to couples after a more respectable interval.[3] However, the circumstances of Shakespeare's marriage are still unusual. He was only eighteen, for instance, when men's mean age at marriage in 1600 (the earliest date it can safely be calculated) was twenty-eight, whereas his bride, Anne Hathaway, was seven or eight years his senior, when women's mean age of marriage was two years younger than their husbands'.[4]

Moreover, the rather tolerant sexual *mores* of the time did not extend generally to families with property. Out of a random sample of sixteen of Stratford's aldermen and capital burgesses in Shakespeare's time, only three appear to have enjoyed their partner's full favours before marriage (or so we may conclude from the precipitate appearance of their first born). Shakespeare's father, as we shall see, though experiencing financial difficulties in the early 1580s, was still an alderman of the borough, and had held the chief civic office, that of high bailiff, in 1568. It is unlikely that the marriage of his eldest son while still a minor was what he had planned for his family. Not, that is, unless his intended bride would have brought a welcome injection of cash into the family. Under her father's will (he had died in September 1581), Anne Hathaway was due to receive £6 13*s* 4*d* on her marriage, not an insubstantial sum but not a fortune either. John Shakespeare, too, despite his financial embarrassment, might have hoped for something better for his eldest son than the daughter of a Shottery husbandman. Much of this is speculation, of course, but the general circumstances of the marriage, especially the couple's ages, do seem unusual against the general background of the time, and it would not be unreasonable to conclude that Shakespeare's marriage might never have taken place had he not made Anne pregnant. Certainly the oft-quoted advice of the Duke in *Twelfth Night* to Viola, disguised as a boy ('Then let thy love be younger than thyself/Or thy affection cannot hold the bent'), suggests he may have regretted his youthful dalliance, or rather that he had not resisted the many pressures to marry the woman he had (for want of a better word) compromised.

Hamnet's burial entry, on 11 August 1596, aged eleven, tells us little, though we may speculate on the general assumption that Shakespeare attended the funeral. If he were in London (or possibly even in Kent, where his company apparently toured that autumn)[5] it is by no means certain that, being summer, the burial would have been put off until his return. From the evidence we have in other cases, a delay of even three days was unusual.[6]

We may also legitimately wonder at this point why Shakespeare had such a small family. Anne first conceived out of wedlock, establishing, one must suppose, a normal fertility, and her second conception followed after not too long an interval. But for the process to stop there was most unusual. A large family was regarded as necessary for a number of reasons, not the least being the assumption that not all children would reach adulthood. We shall see how Shakespeare's improving social position and increasing wealth made a male heir essential if the family's new status was to be maintained. But Shakespeare singularly failed to secure such a succession. All depended on Hamnet's survival, which, as we have just seen, was not to be; and when disaster struck it may have been too late, with Anne approaching forty, to redeem the situation. There are a number of possible explanations, of course. Estrangement is one, but just as likely would be a simple medical reason, such as damage to the reproductive system caused by the carrying and birth of twins, who to have survived at that date are unlikely to have been born prematurely. For the record, however, statistics do not do much to substantiate this. Out of the thirty-two instances of twin births in Stratford between 1560 and 1600, both children survived at least the first three months of infancy in eighteen cases. In ten out of these eighteen cases more children followed, and the real figure may well have been higher, for we cannot be sure that some of the remaining eight households did not move away from the town to complete their families elsewhere.

Shakespeare's burial, on 25 April 1616, is the last of the parish register entries that concern us here, and the only one written not in the hand of the 1600 copyist, but by a man who almost certainly witnessed the event (p. 9). A question that has apparently never been asked, let alone answered, concerns the identity of the man who actually inscribed the words 'Will. Shakespeare gent.' in the register. The answer should be obvious, for the church

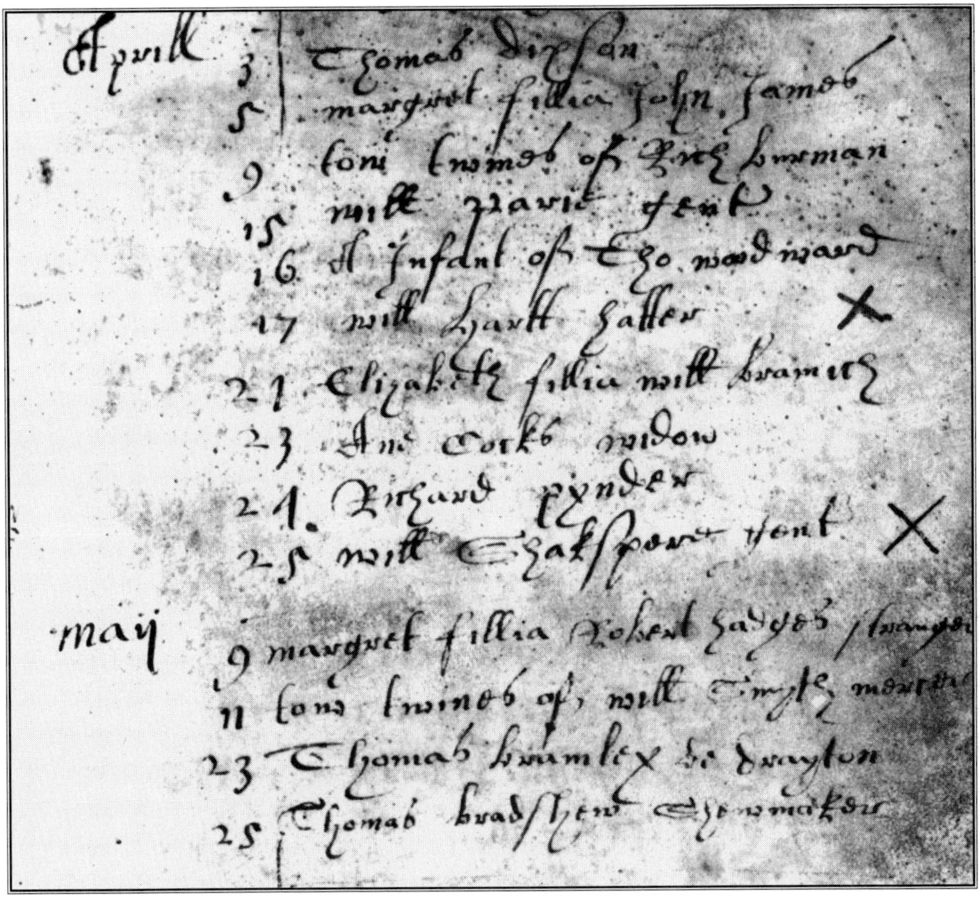

Shakespeare's burial, recorded in the Stratford parish register, 25 April 1616. Shakespeare had died two days previously, probably on his fifty-second birthday. The entry may be in the hand of William Nixon. The other marked entry is for William Hart, hatter, Shakespeare's brother-in-law, who was buried on 17 April. (SBT, DR 243/1, burials, f. 46)

authorities had given clear instructions that the vicar or curate should on Sundays and in the presence of the churchwardens enter up the week's baptisms, marriages and burials, and that each page should be signed as a true record by these same officials. This, however, was not invariably the practice in Stratford. The registers were certainly not compiled by John Rogers, vicar from 1605 to 1619. He was later accused of being too easygoing and only twice (in 1611) signed pages of the register. His curate from October 1613 to May 1617 was Richard Watts and for a few months (June 1614 to March 1615) the register does appear to be in his hand. But before and after this short period another hand was compiling the entries, with Richard Watts and the churchwardens merely signing at the foot of the page. Soon even this observance of formalities was abandoned when for much of 1615 and 1616 the compiler actually wrote in Watts's name (and those of the churchwardens) himself; even more irregular is the complete absence of any signatures at all (forged or otherwise) from the page of burials that contains Shakespeare's name. The situation only improved in 1617 with the appointment of a new curate, Elizeu Owen, who resumed responsibility for keeping the registers.

Such irregularities are entirely consistent with the generally disorganized nature of John Rogers's last years as vicar. Accused by his Puritan enemies of laziness and lack of zeal, he was forcibly replaced by Henry Wilson in 1619. But who had been usurping the duty of compiling the register from 1615 to 1617, not even producing it for inspection? Clues are to be found in the churchwardens' accounts for 1617, the year in which normal practice was restored. In July we read of a payment to one William Nixon 'for his fee' and in October of a further payment to the same man 'for delivering in the regester'.[7] Nixon, with some training in the law, was an official of the local Church court. During the controversy over the dismissal of Rogers, he was variously accused of being part of a conspiracy to unseat Rogers, of forging the signature of the registrar of the consistory court in order to bring Rogers's opponents before the Church courts, and of rioting in the churchyard in an attempt to re-erect a maypole. Such a man may well have appropriated to himself the compiling of the register, unknowingly copying into it one of the most famous burials of all time.

The register, now bearing these momentous entries, continued, of course, in day-to-day use at the parish church. In 1653 it was temporarily laid aside when, under Cromwellian legislation, the keeping of the registers was taken out of the minister's hands and made the responsibility of an elected official. This 'register', as he was rather confusingly called, started a new book, which was handed back to the vicar in 1660 when Cromwell's system was abolished on the restoration of Charles II. By 1687 this volume was full and the vicar then retrieved from the parish chest the original register in order to continue his entries. Its generous proportions served him and his successors for nearly a hundred years, and it was not until 1776 that it was finally filled. It was then put away in the parish chest for safekeeping.

We do not know who first leafed through the pages of this volume looking for Shakespeare entries, but in 1708 Nicholas Rowe, playwright and poet laureate, and engaged in producing an edition of Shakespeare's plays, dispatched the actor Thomas Betterton to Stratford 'on purpose to gather up what remains he could' of Shakespeare's name, which were then worked into a brief biographical preface. Betterton, no antiquarian, made many mistakes, failing for instance to distinguish between two John Shakespeares and thus crediting the poet's father with ten children.

In 1769 the vicar, Stephen Nason, 'faithfully transcribed' from the register the 'births, marriages and burials of the Shakespeare

The Revd James Davenport (1750–1841), vicar of Stratford at the time of Edmond Malone's researches. The silhouette was taken by E.R. Worrall in 1838 on the occasion of the vicar's last sermon. (SBT)

family', sending his notes to David Garrick, then busy with the organization of the jubilee celebrations which were held in Stratford-upon-Avon later that year. Another copy of these notes found its way, via the local headmaster, Joseph Greene, and his antiquarian friend, James West of Alscot Park, to George Steevens, who included them in his contribution to the 1773 edition of Shakespeare's collected works. Nason misread the name of Shakespeare's son Hamnet as Samuel, and similarly made no attempt to distinguish between the John Shakespeares of the day.[8] But in the 1780s there appeared on the scene Edmond Malone, the first scholarly biographer of Shakespeare and a man who will figure frequently in the pages that follow. He was engaged on a new edition of the plays and in April 1788 wrote to the vicar of Stratford, James Davenport, explaining that he wished to revise

Rowe's *Life* as part of this work and asking for one or two details from the register. By the end of the month Davenport had received six such epistles, the last with no less than twelve points on which he needed help. Seeing no end to these escalating demands on his time, Davenport packed the two early registers off to London for Malone to peruse at leisure. This did not put an end to the correspondence and Malone continued to fire off letters to Davenport, announcing his discoveries as he made them. He even took the liberty of having the volumes rebound: 'I prevailed on a bookbinder to come with his tools to me and by vamping them up, putting Russian backs to them etc. he has put them into better plight than they were when I received them.' He returned them at the end of June 1788.[9]

Malone's findings were not in fact published in his new edition of the plays, nor indeed in his lifetime. His ambition had been to write the first Shakespeare biography but although, as we shall see, he subsequently made important discoveries, he never completed his task. His friend, James Boswell (son of Johnson's biographer), published a *Life of Shakespeare* in 1821, working from Malone's notes and previous publications, in which Shakespeare's family details as deduced from the register were eventually sorted out. Other results of his research, however, went unrecorded.

As the nineteenth century progressed more and more visitors came to view Shakespeare's monument in Holy Trinity Church. It then became accepted practice for the sexton to usher visitors into the vestry to view the Shakespeare entries in the register. The increasing wear and tear to which this gave rise led, in 1844, to a need to reback the volume, through the good offices of the parish clerk and amateur bookbinder, Thomas Kite. Then in the mid-1880s it was decided to put the volumes on permanent exhibit in a showcase.[10] This had the desired effect of reducing the handling of the volume but led to a gradual fading of the writing on the crucial pages because of prolonged exposure to the light. In 1966 the vicar and churchwardens made the decision to hand this priceless volume over to the care of the Shakespeare Birthplace Trust. It was once more rebound and placed in the Trust's strongrooms where it was joined by the parish's other registers a few years later: strict controls on humidity and temperature will prevent any further deterioration.

CHAPTER TWO

A Man of Property: Shakespeare's Purchase of New Place

There is no record of substance to throw light on Shakespeare's life and circumstances between the baptism of his twin offspring in 1585 and his resurfacing in London by 1592 as an established playwright. There has been much speculation about how Shakespeare spent these years, but the simplest and most likely theory is that he joined one of the companies of players, whose visits to Stratford are well recorded, and established himself as a writer while performing in their repertory. His success in this field was extraordinary, and by the end of the 1590s we find evidence of a man not only with considerable sums of money to invest in property, but also one anxious to secure his newly won position in society. It was probably he, for instance, who in 1596 established his father's right to bear a coat of arms, and it may also have been out of a desire to make his family's new status clear that he chose to invest his wealth in the purchase of property in Stratford, a town that he had left less than fifteen years before at a time when his family's fortunes were at a very low ebb. In 1597 he bought New Place, with its Great Garden, reputedly the second largest house in Stratford; in 1602 around 120 acres of land in the town's open fields as well as a cottage in Chapel Lane; and in 1605 an interest in part of the town's tithes. His total outlay is not known but could well have exceeded £900 – a very substantial sum at a time when a labourer was fortunate to earn 4*s* a week.[1] One can only speculate on the impression that such an investment by a man still in his early thirties would have had on townsfolk able to recall that Shakespeare's father had been reluctant to leave his house for fear of arrest for debt less than twenty years before.

Among the Shakespeare Birthplace Trust's collections are documents relating to all four of these purchases. The first relates to Shakespeare buying New Place in the spring of 1597 from William Underhill.[2] This, known as an exemplification of a fine, tells us only a part of the story. Originally a deed of conveyance would have accompanied this document, naming the parties involved in more detail, specifying the amount of money that changed hands and describing fully the nature of the property sold. This, unfortunately, has not survived; what we are left with is a record of a fictitious legal action brought in the royal courts, which was the customary way of ensuring that the transaction was registered. Should doubts concerning its validity later arise the court record could be turned up and the details checked. This process was known as a fine, or final concord, which was written out three times on a single piece of parchment and then cut up, one copy (known as the 'foot') remaining in the court's archives and the other two, in theory, being handed over to the vendor and purchaser. It is not, however, any of these that survives at Stratford. The 'foot' is still to be found in the court's records now at the Public Record Office[3] but the purchaser's and vendor's copies, like the deed itself, have also disappeared. Shakespeare, however, had taken the precaution of having a certified copy, or exemplification, made at the same time, bearing the impressive seal of the court. It is this that has come down to us (p 17).

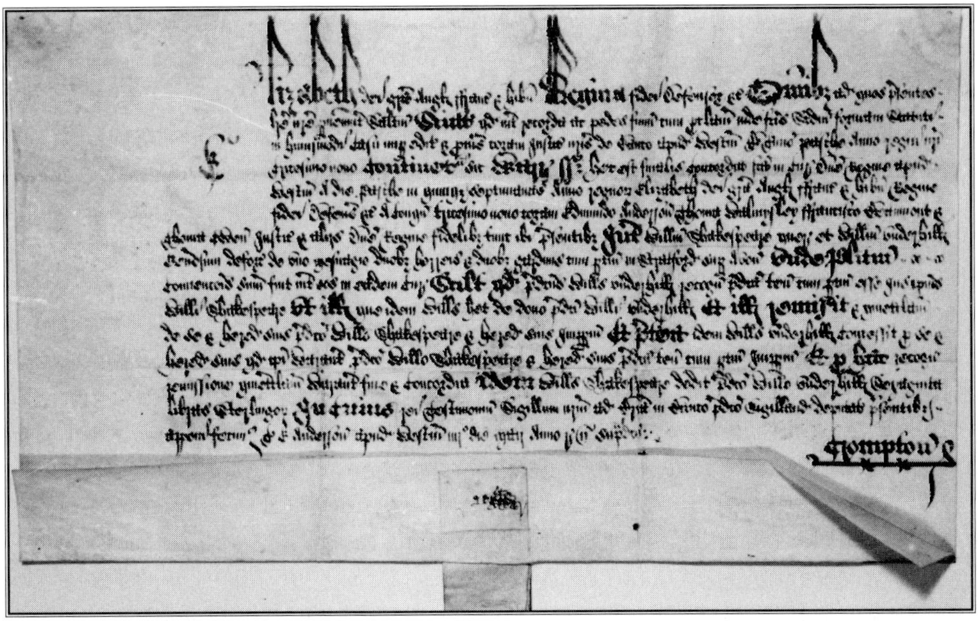

The imposing exemplification, issued in the name of Queen Elizabeth on 4 May 1597, of the fine recording Shakespeare's purchase of New Place from William Underhill. The conveyance which went with it (now lost) would have been dated a few weeks earlier. (SBT, ER 27/4a)

It is well worth asking why Shakespeare went to these lengths, for exemplifications of fines are, in fact, far from common. Most people were evidently satisfied to receive just the standard copies and only too ready to forgo the more costly process of securing an exemplification. Certainly an exemplification was a more impressive document to produce if a dispute did ensue, but we know of no reason, when Shakespeare made the purchase, to anticipate trouble and, even if there had been, his deed and his purchaser's fine would have been sufficient to prove title. It could be, however, that Shakespeare, like the other 'new' gentry of his time, was indulging in a little harmless snobbery. There are many other examples of middle-class families who invested their money in lands that had come on to the market following the dissolution of the monasteries. They then had their title to these secured by elaborate certified copies of their deeds,[4] and kept the College of Heralds busy by making tenuous claims to a right to bear a coat of arms in order to secure entry into the élite band of gentry. We cannot assume that Shakespeare was above such things.

One or two further points should be made about this document. It does not, for instance, describe the property as New Place. As was the custom in documents of this sort, the details are formalized and we read only of a house, two barns and two gardens. It is only because we know that William Underhill bought New Place in 1567 and that when Shakespeare died in 1616 he was the owner of the same property, that we can safely infer that this exemplification does indeed record its conveyance from one family to the other. The original that went with the fine would have made this clear, of course, but as we have seen it has not survived. Nor does it record the actual sum of money that changed hands. A sum of £60 is mentioned, but it has long been recognized that this, as with other sums that fines and final concords record, was not what was actually paid: it was, like the legal action itself, a fiction. In 1563, when William Clopton sold New Place to William Bott, £140 change hands, and in 1567, when it was sold on to William Underhill, £110 (or apparently so: the deed is damaged at the vital part).[5] We may assume therefore that in 1597 Shakespeare would have paid a sum roughly within these limits. We might note at this point, therefore, that there are many instances where the amount specified in a fine is exactly half that mentioned in the actual deed of conveyance. One cannot make too much of this, as it is equally true that there are as many instances when this is not the case; but if Shakespeare did indeed pay £120 for New Place, it is about the sum one might have expected.

At this point we should consider a much neglected document which tells us a good deal about the extent of Shakespeare's New Place property. The house itself stood on the corner of Chapel Street and Chapel Lane, and in medieval times its garden would have run back down the latter some 180 ft or so. Beyond this were the holdings of various religious and charitable foundations. The first belonged to a chantry at Ettington church and dog-legged out, apparently, into Chapel Street, through what is now part of the Shakespeare Hotel.[6] Next came land in the possession of Pinley Priory, then a 30 ft by 180 ft plot held by the parish of Clifford Chambers for charitable purposes, and finally land held by the Abbey of Reading. One by one these four holdings were added to the New Place estate to create the Great Garden as we know it today (p. 20).

The two easterly plots were added as late as 1758[7] and were therefore never part of Shakespeare's holdings. But the other two were, a fact that can be deduced from a lease of the Clifford property in 1572. On the back of this was scrawled, at a later date, a note to the effect that the propety adjoining it on the west was a barn formerly belonging to Pinley Priory but now to William Shakespeare.[8] It is difficult to be precise about the date of this note. Clearly it predates Shakespeare's death in April 1616, and must also be later than March 1603 as it continues with a note that the land abutting on the other side was then held by the king (that is, James I rather than Queen Elizabeth). What is certain, however, is that only the plot of land formerly belonging to Pinley Priory (and presumably the other plot between it and New Place) ever

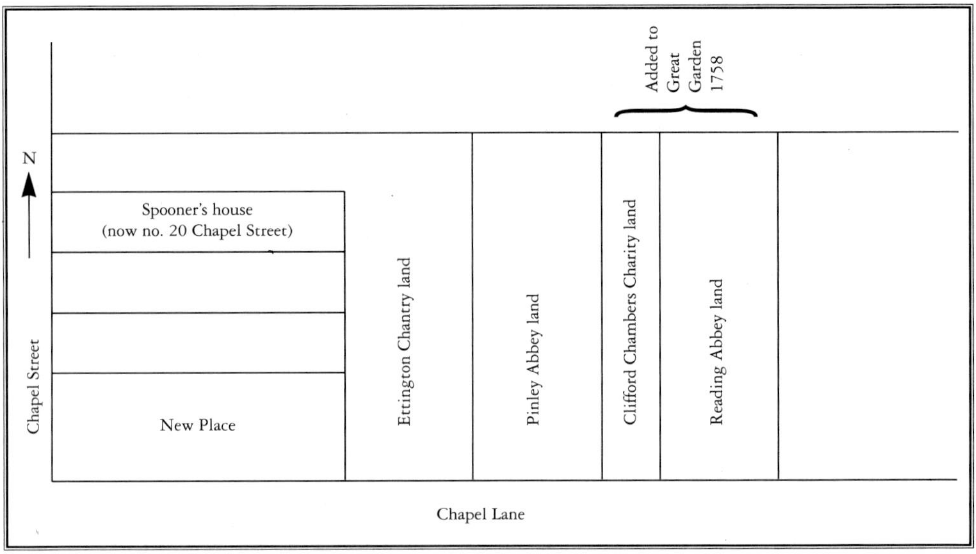

Diagram to illustrate the plots of land in Chapel Lane, later to form the Great Garden of New Place

belonged to Shakespeare. Quite what proportion of the present Great Garden this represents is uncertain. The Clifford property was 30 ft wide and the Reading Abbey land (which also had room for a barn) may have been as much as 60 ft wide. This would reduce the present Great Garden by over a third.

When we turn to examine the date that the Ettington and Pinley holdings may have been added to New Place, we find, apparently, that this had not occurred by February 1563; for in a deed of that date, whereby New Place was conveyed by William Clopton to William Bott, the abutting property at the bottom of the plot was described as a barn lately belonging to Ettington chantry.[9] Just over two years later, however, in June 1565, Bott accused one Richard Spooner (living in what is now No. 20 Chapel Street) of breaking into his 'barne yarde . . . *iuxta* [next to] New Place gardyn' in Chapel Lane to remove pieces of timber.[10] This would seem to be a sure indication that Bott had bought at least the Ettington chantry land running along the back of both his and Spooner's property since acquiring New Place. A survey of 1590 also shows Underhill, to whose father Bott sold New Place in 1567, in possession not only of New Place itself but of a barn in Chapel Lane.[11] This same survey goes on to list a barn held by the heirs of William Smith (he had died in 1578) and then the barn belonging to Clifford Chambers parish. Could it be, then, that the Pinley Abbey property had passed since the Dissolution to William Smith, but that by 1590 it was still not part of the New Place estate? If so, then Underhill almost certainly bought it before selling New Place to Shakespeare, as the final concord for the sale, which we have already discussed, mentions not only a house but also *two* barns. Not too much emphasis should perhaps be placed on this, as the language of fines is highly formalized; nevertheless it is a material fact that cannot be entirely ignored. The alternative, which is not impossible, is that Shakespeare himself bought the Pinley property from the Smiths before the rough note was written on the back of the Clifford lease.

CHAPTER THREE

Shakespeare and the Stratford Corporation: the Quiney Letters and the 'Noate of Corn and Malt'

Shakespeare's remarkable financial success and the investment in a substantial property in his native town brought him and his family back into contact with the ruling oligarchy there. Shakespeare's father, John, as we have seen, had played an important part in civic affairs in the 1560s and early 1570s, but had then run into difficulties. From 1576 he stopped attending council meetings and was eventually removed from the aldermen's bench ten years later. From 1578 he began mortgaging parts of his wife's estate, and there is other evidence of increasing indebtedness. By 1591 he was even absenting himself from church for fear of arrest by his creditors if he stepped outside his house. His son's success, however, more than compensated for the family's temporary fall from grace. The purchase of New Place, built by the local squire and the residence of gentlemen for a hundred years, was a fitting sequel to the family's acquisition of a coat of arms the previous year. Such activities would have been beyond the normal aspirations of the tradesmen families who dominated the

Corporation. But the Shakespeares' case was an unusual one, and transformed a family that for some years had been fighting a losing battle to maintain its position within the business community into one that the borough authorities would have to court if its influence were to be used in the town's favour. Wealthy allies were at a premium in the late 1590s.

Since 1553, when Stratford was granted its Charter of Incorporation, the town had been governed by a self-electing body of twenty-four aldermen and capital burgesses presided over by a high bailiff. The Corporation's first members were named in the charter, and the vacancies that occurred later were filled on the nomination of the existing members. In such circumstances its membership quickly came to reflect the principal trading interests in the town. Its main statutory duty was to administer the income from the very considerable property with which it was endowed in order to maintain the grammar school, administer the almshouses and pay the vicar. This it certainly did, but in the performance of these tasks it should not really come as a surprise to find that the management of its estates was carried out with an eye to the advantage of the members of the Corporation (the granting of leases to themselves is an obvious example) and that the town's interests, which it strove to promote or fought to defend, also represented their own.

By the 1590s these interests were threatened by a severe economic crisis.[1] In 1594 and 1595 two devastating fires destroyed 200 dwellings in the town centre, rendering 400 people dependent on poor relief and causing an alleged £20,000 worth of damage. A succession of bad harvests in the mid-1590s led, in Stratford-upon-Avon as in most urban centres, to a severe shortage of corn, near famine conditions and stirrings of rebellion.[2] By 1601 the Stratford authorities were claiming that 700 people (roughly a third of the population) were officially registered as paupers. Their measures to combat the crisis may seem draconian, but were common practice throughout the country. Vagrants were denied entry to the town and newcomers driven out. Fines were imposed on those harbouring 'strangers and inmates' and attempts were made to control 'tippling houses', the customary haunt of the poorer classes. Attempts were also made (of particular relevance in the context of Shakespeare's relationship with the Corporation) to increase the town's revenues by securing a new charter and to seek exemption from central government taxation, which bore heavily on the well-to-do of the town who were having to foot the bill for keeping the town's paupers. The Corporation also petitioned strongly against government legislation to restrict the malting industry, introduced from 1594 in an attempt to ensure that the barley crop was not frittered away during a period of severe food shortage. This, it was alleged, hit business interests hard, as 'our town hath no other especial trade' and 'our houses are fitted to no other uses'.[3]

To ensure that the town's case was properly heard by the government in London, it was necessary from time to time for the Corporation to dispatch one of its number to the capital. As often as not its choice fell on a leading mercer in the town, Richard Quiney. In 1595 he is found presenting the evidence of the effects on the town of the two fires; in February 1597 he was back to prosecute a suit against William Underhill; over the winter 1597/8 he returned to argue the town's case for a new charter; and the following winter (1598/9) he reappeared to seek exemption from the latest tax subsidy and the malting restrictions.[4]

Our present interest in these London visits lies in the bundle of precious letters he received from Stratford and the notes he made concerning his expenses. Most of these he carefully preserved and, on his untimely death in 1602, while serving a second term as bailiff, they passed into the Corporation archives. Two hundred years later, as we shall see, they were unearthed by Shakespeare scholars. Among the documents were discovered four which mentioned Shakespeare, including the only surviving letter addressed to him; and together they also set in context another document containing mention of the poet, the so-called 'noate of corn and malt' of 1598.

These letters prove that while in London Quiney saw or made contact with Shakespeare at least once. No doubt they met on other occasions too. This has often been interpreted as evidence of friendship, but is just as likely, as already suggested, to have arisen out of the Corporation's anxiety to seek the favour of this new man of substance. It is in this light that the references to Shakespeare can be most easily interpreted.

There is no evidence of a meeting between the two men until the 1597/8 visit, but we may speculate that contact was made during Quiney's visit of February 1597. On this occasion he had been sent to London in pursuit of some back rent owed to the Corporation by William Underhill, described as a 'subtle, crafty and covetous man'. It may be coincidence, but a few weeks later William Underhill sold New Place to Shakespeare. It would have indeed suited all parties if Quiney had put Shakespeare up to this purchase. Underhill was pressed for cash, the Corporation was in dire need of funds to support the town's poor, and Shakespeare had money to invest. In these circumstances he would have been well placed to strike a bargain, favourable to himself and Stratford's governing body.

If this is to some extent speculation, we are on firmer ground during Quiney's 1597/8 visit, for in a letter written to him from Stratford on 24 January 1598 by his friend and fellow burgess Abraham Sturley, occurs the first of our four references to

Shakespeare.[5] He tells Quiney of the understanding in the town that Shakespeare, clearly on the lookout for further investment, was interested in 'some odd yardland [about 30 acres] or other at Shottery'; the advice he gives, however, is that Shakespeare should be persuaded to invest instead in a lease of the Corporation tithes. Quiney was to point out 'the friends he can make therefore' and how it would 'advance him indeed'. At the same time it 'would do us [i.e. the Corporation] much good'. In other words, as with the purchase of New Place (if we are correct in our assumption that a deal was struck on that occasion), both sides would benefit. Quiney, however, either did not pursue the matter or was unsuccessful when he made his proposal to Shakespeare. As we shall see, it was not until 1605 that he invested in the Stratford tithes, and then only after he had bought other property.

This same letter then goes on to give fascinating background information to the so-called 'noate of corn and malt', drawn up days later, in which Shakespeare also figures. The bad harvests, Sturley continues, were causing unprecedented discontent: 'You shall understand that our neighbours are grown with the wants they feel through the dearness of corn (which here is beyond all other countries that I can hear of dear and over-dear) malcontent; they have assembled together in a great number and travelled to Sir Thomas Lucy [a local Justice of the Peace] to complain of our maltsters. . . . The Lord knoweth to what end it will sort . . .'. One of the protesters had declared that 'he hoped within a week to lead some of them in a halter, meaning the maltsters'. Another declared: 'I hope . . . to see them hanged on gibbets at their own doors.' Clearly the populace, in Stratford as elsewhere across the country, was close to open rebellion and Sturley pleads: 'I would write nothing unto you but come home.'

To put these remarks in context we need to return to 1595, the year the bad harvests began. The government had not been unresponsive. In order to alleviate the hardships suffered by the poorer classes as a result of the severe food shortages, investigations had been authorized to ascertain who was hoarding corn and malt with the intention of releasing it on to the market at inflated prices. Malt was produced from barley and used extensively for brewing, and in an effort to save the crop for food the Justices of the Peace were also given powers to limit the industry. In Stratford forty-four maltsters were bound over to cease malting on 4 November 1595, and shortly afterwards the statutory investigation into those hoarding grain was carried out. The results survive in two remarkable documents now in the Warwick Castle archives, where they form part of the papers of Sir Fulke Greville, Justice of the Peace and Deputy Lieutenant for the county, to whom, we may assume, the task of collecting this information had been delegated. Both Sturley and Quiney came out badly in the report, being described as 'great corn buyers and buyers of wood and such like' – Quiney, in particular, 'useth the trades of buying and selling of corn for great sums and making of malt'. He was alleged to have in his barn 47 quarters of barley and 32 quarters of malt, besides other produce, making him by far the worst offender. Sturley, with 26 quarters of malt, was also listed as a corn dealer and maltster.[6]

The food crisis of 1597/8 was worse than any that had gone before. The price of wheat had risen from about 17*s* a quarter in 1592 to a record high of over 50*s* by 1596.[7] In 1597 the death rate in Stratford-upon-Avon soared to over twice the usual rate as diseases associated with malnutrition took their toll.[8] The government continued to press for measures to outlaw hoarding, and authorized further inquisitions in August 1597, the Privy Council regretfully concluding that these hoarders ('wicked people in conditions more like to wolves') included in their number 'men which are of good livelihood and in estimation of worship'.[9] The local outcome of this new drive was the Stratford 'noate of corn and malt', taken on 4 February 1598.[10]

One of the most intriguing features of this document, in addition of course to its reference to Shakespeare, is the fact that it is in Quiney's handwriting. Even allowing that this may be an official copy made a few days after the event, he must clearly have taken heed of Sturley's plea and hurried home, knowing full well that if the charges of two years ago were repeated, his property might well be vulnerable to attack. Sturley's letter, written on 24 January, can hardly have reached him before 27 January, yet here he is in Stratford a few days later taking a leading part in the investigation. Gone, too, from this account is the bitter language of the 1595 survey, and the huge stocks then reported have shrunk miraculously. Quiney himself now holds only 14 quarters of malt (instead of his 1595 total of 79 quarters of barley and malt); Sturley's holding has dropped to an even more modest 5 quarters; and John Rogers, another hoarder against whom serious charges had been laid in 1595, is found now to have only 7 quarters compared to his earlier total of 37 quarters.

Can these figures be taken at their face value, or had those with most to lose this time made sure, by compiling the survey themselves, that the criticisms of them in 1595 would not be repeated? While this would seem more than a possibility, more to the point is the clear conviction of those suffering severe deprivation that there *was* grain in the town. This belief, whether justified or not, was, like others of its kind, a threat to civil order and to the interests of the propertied class; and the 1598 survey, clearly supervised this time by the Corporation and with its plain statement of fact (or alleged fact) seems to have been intended to reduce tension. We also know, incidentally, that Quiney and

Sturley were quite happy to speculate in barley, as the following year one wrote to the other: 'If you have any to spare [i.e. cash], in barley is the surest profit, by which if you had been at home you should have gained more than by all your travail.'[11]

Accurate or not, we have still to consider the inclusion of Shakespeare's name. He was absent from the earlier survey, not then being a Stratford householder, but his purchase of New Place in May 1597 made him a leading figure in the town; and in the 1598 'noate of corn and malt', under Church and Chapel Street ward in which New Place lay, we find him listed as the owner of 10 quarters (p. 30). Though this figure, like the others in the survey, may be open to some doubt, certain observations can still be made. Firstly, Shakespeare had clearly not been slow, since his purchase of the property the previous May, in stocking up in a valuable commodity – further evidence of the availability of ready cash. At current prices his reported holding (and it may have been an underestimate) would have been worth over £25 at a time, as we have seen, when a labourer's weekly wage was only 4*s*. Secondly, his prosperity, relative to that of others in the town, can be roughly assessed by comparing his 10 quarters with the other holdings listed: for, of the seventy-five burgesses in the survey, only thirteen were reported to have held more than Shakespeare. At a time when thousands of his compatriots were in desperate need of food (and indeed in many cases were on the verge of starvation), Shakespeare must surely have been as fearful as other civic leaders that he could be a target during any civil disturbance. Many have interpreted the opening scene of *Coriolanus*, portraying riots in Rome due to grain shortages, as evidence of Shakespeare's first-hand experience of similar events in his own lifetime. General unrest in 1607 and 1608 is usually cited in support of this, coinciding with the generally accepted date for the writing of the play. The 1597/8 disorders, however, are a better

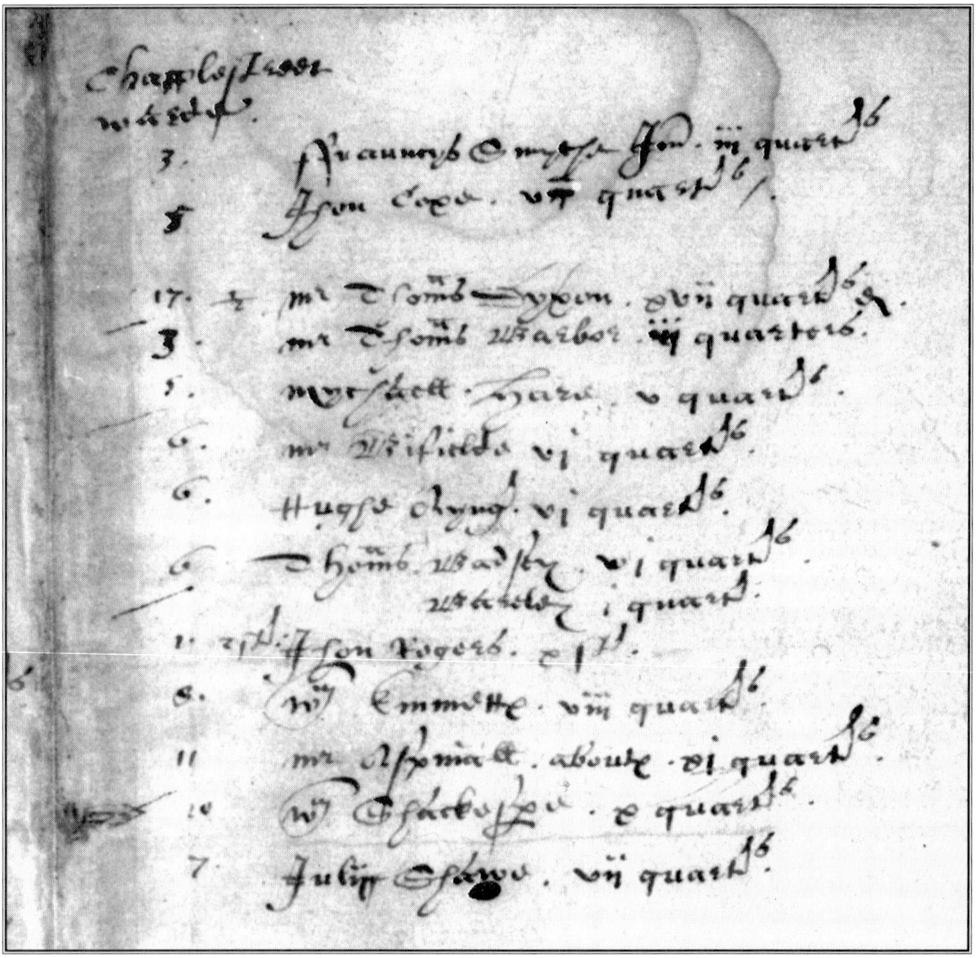

Part of the survey, 4 February 1598, of those in Stratford hoarding corn and malt. Shakespeare, with 10 quarters, is listed under Chapel Street ward in which New Place lay. The hand is Richard Quiney's. (SBT, BRU 15/1/106)

example of Shakespeare's direct link with the type of events that *Coriolanus* depicts.

This is not the only time that we hear of Shakespeare in possession of malt surplus to his own requirements, for in another important document we find the dramatist, in 1604, pursuing the apothecary Philip Rogers through the local courts to recover a debt incurred when, in the spring of that year, he had sold him 20 bushels of malt.[12] On the face of it there is nothing extraordinary in this. The proceedings of Stratford's Court of Record, with jurisdiction over debts up to £30, is full of similar cases brought by the town's trading fraternity against defaulters. Indeed one could argue that Shakespeare's name might well have been expected to have occurred more often; as it is, the Rogers case and a similar one brought against John Addenbrooke in 1608[13] are the only occasions on which Shakespeare used the Court of Record in his business dealings. But it is worthy of remark that in just this one deal with Rogers Shakespeare had disposed of 20 bushels, equivalent to a quarter of his 1598 holding. Assuming there were other sales of which no records survive (as would be the case if payment were duly made), it is difficult to see this transaction as, to quote a recent source, similar to those made by a man 'with more than sufficient malt for his domestic brewing' who 'sometimes parted with a few bushels of corn on credit'.[14] At the very least it would suggest that Shakespeare had the necessary means to invest in the purchase of quantities of grain well in excess of his needs. Whether this was a precaution against possible shortages, or whether it was done with a deliberate eye for resale, we cannot, however, tell.

The other three Quiney letters that contain references to Shakespeare concern not the Corporation affairs but the personal finances of Quiney himself, and in all probability those of his friend Sturley as well. Sturley hailed from Worcester, but following a period at Cambridge University he married a Stratford girl in 1575 and settled in the town five years later. An attorney by profession, but with a number of other business interests, he was elected a capital burgess in 1591 and served as high bailiff in 1596. By 1597, however, he and, to a lesser extent, Quiney were in financial difficulties. This was due in part to the casual way in which the town's financial affairs were managed and the tendency for private business dealings to become inextricably mixed up with those transacted on behalf of the Corporation. Quiney, for instance, was one of the burgesses sent out to other parts of the country to collect money for the relief of the town after the fires of 1594 and 1595. Such collections, though they needed royal sanction, were a recognized means of meeting some of the victims' compensation claims. But it is clear that much of the money that Quiney collected never passed through the Corporation's hands, but was dispensed by him directly to claimants. He also used some of this 'fire money' for his expenses while on his 1597/8 visit to London, claiming that out of the £75 6*s* 0*d* he had received in Norfolk and Suffolk he only owed the Corporation £20 16*s* 8*d*.[15] In his letters to Quiney, Sturley also refers to the setting of expenses against the Corporation debts.[16] These included, no doubt, a sum of £50 that the Corporation was claiming Quiney owed them in January 1596 and a further £20 allegedly due from Sturley. By June Quiney had reduced his debt to £10 but Sturley's remained at £20, and the Corporation, getting impatient, insisted that the two men enter into bonds to guarantee repayment by January next.[17] A letter from Sturley to Quiney on 4 November 1597 reveals his increasing embarrassment. Reporting on the pressing demands of a creditor, he exclaims: 'To what purpose or with what heart can a man, grieved and burdened with his wants, satisfy him that would fain have money when he has nothing but words to pay him withall?'[18] On 8 November he again wrote to Quiney asking for assistance in heading off a creditor,[19] and by 24 January 1598 confided that he was 'left I assure you in the greatest need of £30 that possibly may be: in truth, brother, to you be it spoken and to no else, for want thereof know scarce which way to turn me'.[20] Two paragraphs later he referred to £80 that he had borrowed from a London money-lender, to be repaid the following May, and asked Quiney to try and have the repayment of £40 of it deferred for six months.[21] At this point Quiney, as we have seen, hurried home on the news of impending food riots, but on his return to London in the autumn of 1598 the resumption of their correspondence shows that Sturley's troubles were far from over. In a letter of 16 October we learn that a bond for £100 was due for payment on 22 November and he was also in urgent need of £25 to meet pressing creditors, which he hoped 'might by your [Quiney's] good labour and leisure be procured'.[22]

This, then, is the background to one of the most intriguing Shakespeare documents to have survived, the letter that Quiney wrote a few days later, on 25 October, from his inn in London, asking Shakespeare for help with a loan of £30.[23] Ostensibly this was 'to help me of all the debts I owe in London', yet it is difficult not to link the request with Sturley's difficulties and in particular with his plea for £25 made a few days before. Quiney comes straight to the point with his 'loving good friend and countryman', 'craving' in the first sentence of the letter 'your help with £30'. Such familiarity must surely give substance to the assumption that the two men had met on a fairly regular basis during Quiney's previous London trips. A request for £30 is also indicative of Shakespeare's ample means, or at least of the means that he was believed to possess. At a time when a house could change hands for less, this was no trifling sum.

The letter was folded and sealed but not, it seems, dispatched – or so we may assume from the fact that it was discovered in Quiney's own papers (p. 35). We can only speculate about what actually happened. It has been suggested that Quiney may instead have met Shakespeare that day, by accident or design, making a letter redundant. Alternatively Quiney may just have decided not to seek help for a loan, although this, as we shall see, seems unlikely. It is even possible that Shakespeare returned the letter, enclosed in his reply. What we do know, however, is that before the day was out Quiney sat down and wrote another letter, this one to Sturley. Regrettably this has not survived, but we know he wrote it, for Sturley refers to 'the letter of 25 of October' when he replied to it on 4 November.[24] He was pleased to hear 'that our countriman Mr. Wm. Shak. would procure us money, which I will like of as I shall hear when, and where, and how, and I pray let not go that occasion if it may sort to any indifferent conditions. Also that if money might be had for £30 or £40, a lease etc might be procured. Oh, how can you make doubt of money, who will not bear xxx*s* or xl*s*. towards such a match.'

This intriguing passage (though it would be more intelligible if we had Quiney's letter) tells us several important things. Firstly, it would seem to establish that the approach to Shakespeare was indeed made on Sturley's and Quiney's joint behalf ('would procure *us* money'). Secondly, though a deal had clearly not been clinched, it would certainly seem that negotiations had begun and that, even if Shakespeare had not received Quiney's note, contact must indeed have been made on 25 October. The final two sentences, though difficult to interpret precisely, clearly hint at the terms on which a loan might be secured. As early as 1848 J.O. Halliwell pointed out that they could be taken as evidence of Shakespeare lending money at interest, and this has been advocated more vigorously in recent years by Professor Ernst Honigmann, drawing on the discovery that Shakespeare's father, John, had himself been prosecuted for lending money at illegally high rates of interest.[25] Certainly Quiney's own letter

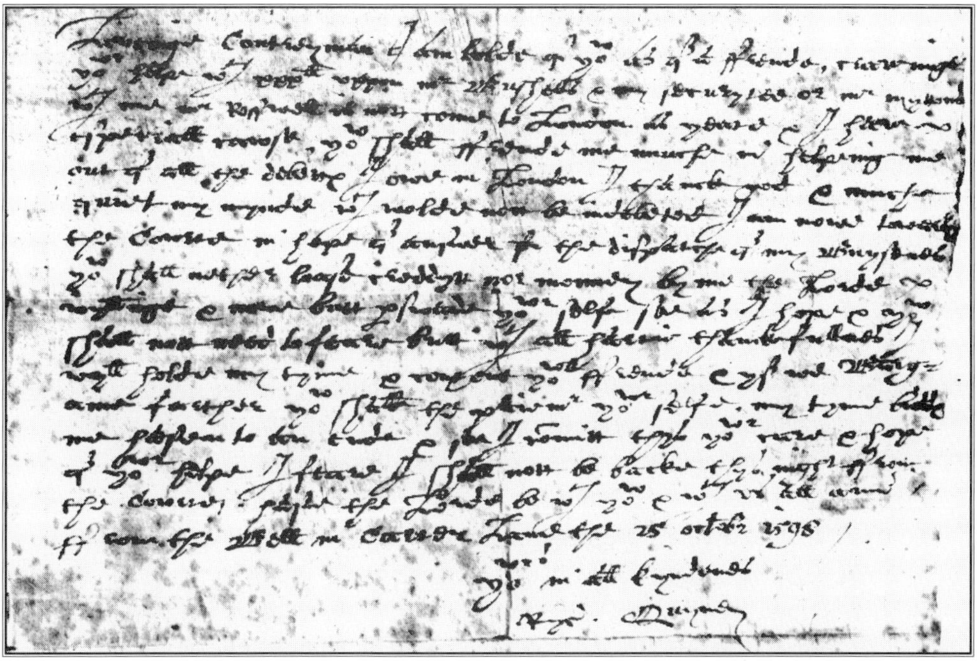

Richard Quiney's letter to William Shakespeare asking for help with a loan of £30; 25 October 1598. The paper on which it was written was then folded and sealed and the address written on the back. (SBT, ER 27/4)

suggests at one point that Shakespeare himself would be the creditor ('You shall neither lose credit nor money by me'), but on the other hand he goes on to refer to a possible third party ('I will hold my time [i.e. repay by an agreed date] and content your friend'). Sturley's letter, in referring to the offer to 'procure' money, also suggests that Shakespeare was acting only as an intermediary, though the possible terms (30*s* or 40*s* interest on a loan of £30 or £40) had evidently led to some dithering on Quiney's part. Moreover, money-lending, though legalized in 1591, was still not entirely respectable and was in any case a risky undertaking unless professionally managed. Shakespeare, on receiving Quiney's request, is perhaps more likely to have sought to use his influence by approaching a professional third party, and on balance the correspondence can be more easily interpreted in this light.

Sturley evidently made Quiney's negotiations with Shakespeare known to his immediate acquaintance, for about the same time Quiney received a note from his father, Adrian, full of family news but advising him that 'if you bargain with Mr. Shakespeare or receive money there', then he should buy such items as he might later sell for profit, recommending in particular knit hose which were then changing hands cheaply at Evesham.[26] Daniel Baker, Quiney's nephew, had also found out from his aunt about the proposed deal. He wrote, on 24 November: 'My aunt Quiney [i.e. Richard Quiney's wife] telleth me that you are to receive £20 or £30 in London, and that you will pay some money for me if need be; and in that respect I have lent her some money already to serve her occasions.'[27]

These letters, then, and the 'noate of corn and malt', demonstrate clearly how Shakespeare's recently acquired affluence and his obvious interest in investing in property in his native town made him, to the civic leaders, a man worth knowing. Nor was he unresponsive, and over the next few years he made further substantial purchases in the town.

CHAPTER FOUR

Shakespeare the Gentleman: Further Purchases in Stratford

In 1602 Shakespeare made two investments in local property. New Place stood on the corner of Chapel Street and Chapel Lane with its garden running back down the latter. Opposite, on the other side of Chapel Lane (now occupied by Grammar School buildings), was a piece of land belonging to the manor of Rowington. Rowington itself is some 8 miles north of Stratford and this land (and another piece in Church Street) still remained under its theoretical jurisdiction as part of the lands of the former Abbey of Reading. When the tenancy of such a piece of land changed hands it was necessary for the outgoing tenant, or his legal representative, to appear in the manor court to surrender his holding into the lord's hands and for the new tenant, usually at the same court, to receive it back. This transaction would be duly recorded on the manor rolls as part of that court's proceedings and a copy made of the relevant passage, which was then handed to the new tenant. His title was thus secured by copy of court roll, hence the term 'copyholder'.

In 1602 the copyholder of the Chapel Lane property was Walter Getley, with whom Shakespeare had evidently negotiated a transfer. On 28 September Getley therefore appeared at the manor court and surrendered the land in question into the lord's hands. If the transaction had followed its normal course Shakespeare would then have appeared to be granted possession of it. In fact this did not happen. Shakespeare, perhaps in London, failed to make arrangements for an attorney to act for him and the court roll merely recorded that the land would be held by the lord of the manor until Shakespeare came to take possession. A copy of this transaction, though incomplete, was still made and duly became Shakespeare's title deed. It survives to this day and, because the original manor rolls are no longer extant, provides us with our only knowledge of the deal.[1]

There is no doubt that Shakespeare's title to this property was regarded as valid, even though there is no evidence that he ever formally appeared at the manor court to receive the land out of the lord's hands. It is, for instance, one of the properties mentioned in his will. Nevertheless, when in 1606 a survey of the manor was made the compiler was aware of the irregularity. For although he duly entered Shakespeare as the tenant he was unable to find the date of the court at which Shakespeare was admitted and so left a blank space.[2] Clearly the formalities had not been properly observed.

Two documents survive concerning the next purchase.[3] On 1 May 1602 Shakespeare bought from William Combe and his nephew John, two local gentlemen, 107 acres of land in the open fields to the north and east of the town for £320. In the early days of conveyancing it was customary for a deed of sale to be written out twice on a single sheet of parchment, which was then cut in two along an indented line (hence the term 'indenture'), one copy being given to the purchaser and the other to the vendor. In the event of a subsequent dispute forgery could be proved (or disproved) by bringing the two halves together to check whether they matched. In addition, the vendor's copy would be signed by the purchaser and vice versa.

Of the two documents concerning Shakespeare's 1602 purchase, one is clearly the purchaser's copy. It is signed and sealed by William Combe and John Combe, with five further signatures of those present. Shakespeare himself was not there, but he had appointed his brother Gilbert to act for him and to take receipt of the deed. We have already seen, when considering the Chapel Lane purchase, that Shakespeare had not been in Stratford in September of that year; nor was he, apparently, in May.

This period of absence, probably in London, may explain the other document that has survived. This has all the outward appearance of being the vendor's copy. Its wording is identical to the purchaser's, it is in the same hand, and it was originally sealed. If we are correct in our supposition, it should also have borne Shakespeare's signature and those of the witnesses. But it does not. This could be explained, of course, by Shakespeare's absence. The counterpart, awaiting his signature, could easily have been forgotten about or never asked for by the Combes, and filed away instead with Shakespeare's own copy. There is, however, another possibility. The vendor's copy, if such it is, is not a true counterpart. It is narrower than the one that the Combes signed and the indented top edges do not match. It also contains an error, for the scribe had to go back and insert a clause, though not an important one. It is therefore just possible that other copies had to be drawn out, but the rejected one was nevertheless retained.

Something of the earlier history of the land referred to here has been known for some time,[4] it having been traced as passing from the Clopton family to one Rice Griffin in 1571 and from him to John Combe in 1593. However, a recently discovered document not only adds to our knowledge of these transactions but also describes the property in minute detail and tells us something of its later history.[5] Around 1625 Simon Archer, lord of the manor of Bishopton, was making enquiries into a rent charge of 26*s* 8*d* due to him from certain lands in Clopton. Research revealed that these had been the subject of an exchange in 1542 between William Clopton and the then lord of Bishopton, Sir Richard Catesby, and that this property had then been 'sold by Mr. William Clopton . . . to one Mr. Ryce Griffin, he sold to Mr. J. Combe, Mr. Combe sold it to William Shakespeare who had one daughter and gave the said land with his daughter in marriage to Mr. Hall of Stratford who hath now all the said lands'. The same document describes the land in detail, confirming, as suspected, that it lay scattered in the old unenclosed fields to the north of the town. These fields were

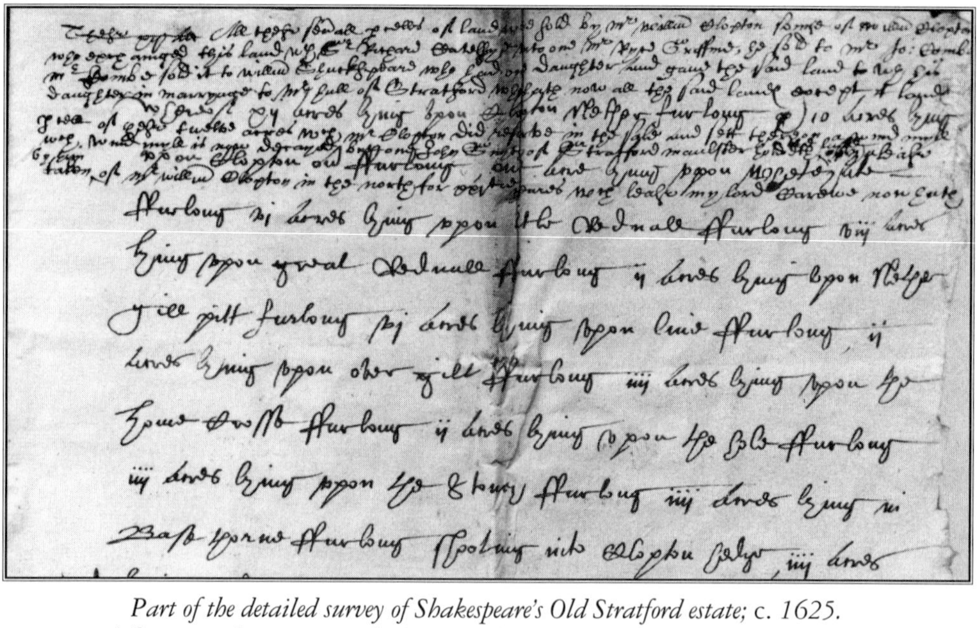

Part of the detailed survey of Shakespeare's Old Stratford estate; c. 1625. *The cramped insertion at the top gives the history of the ownership of the land and the remainder the location of the parcels of which it was comprised lying scattered through the common fields. (SBT, DR 37/Box 113/15)*

subdivided into irregularly shaped 'furlongs' and Shakespeare's holdings were distributed through nineteen of these. Some were near the edge of the town, for instance, in 'Nether Gill Pitt Furlong', which must have been near the Guild Pits, or Guild Street as it is now known. Some were at 'Top of Rowley' and 'Under Rowley' (the rising ground after which Rowley Crescent and the Rowley Estate were named). Ten acres were on the other side of Warwick Road, in the water-meadows there (p. 40).

Another intriguing fact to emerge from this document is the reference to the settlement of these lands on his daughter, Susanna, when she married John Hall in 1607. Not too much should perhaps be made of this, firstly because the informant is incorrect in saying that Susanna was Shakespeare's only daughter, and secondly because the lands in question were still in Shakespeare's hands when he bequeathed them to Susanna by his will of 1616. On the other hand, we must assume that a marriage settlement of some sort was negotiated in 1607 and, if it had included these 107 acres, it would have been usual for Shakespeare to have retained a life interest in these lands. The failure to mention Shakespeare's other daughter, Judith, is less easily explained. She had married Thomas Quiney in 1616 and apparently was still living in Stratford when this document was drawn up.[6] It has long been recognized, however, that the marriage may not have been to Shakespeare's liking. The alterations he made to his will after his new son-in-law was cited for adultery in the ecclesiastical court must surely indicate distrust, and Quiney's subsequent career reveals a wayward disposition.[7] It is not impossible, then, that Judith's unfortunate liaison with the younger son of a vintner had effectively removed her from public notice.

The final title deed we need to consider is Shakespeare's purchase of a share in the Stratford tithes which he bought from Ralph Hubaud of Ipsley in 1605 for £440. Tithes originated as a payment to the rector of a parish of a tenth part of agricultural produce. Over the years the right to the tithes of some parishes passed into the hands of monasteries and other religious houses who appointed a vicar and paid him out of the proceeds. When these foundations were suppressed during the reigns of Henry VIII and Edward VI the rights to such tithes passed, with their other possessions, into the Crown's hands and were then liable to be sold off in the same way as any other piece of property. In the case of Stratford, the tithes had been appropriated in the Middle Ages by the college of priests attached to Holy Trinity Church. When, at the Reformation, this college was suppressed, the ownership of part of the tithes (those of Old Stratford, Bishopton and Welcombe, and the lesser tithes of the whole parish) was granted to the newly incorporated borough.

The owners of tithes at this period rarely collected them themselves. Instead, for a fixed sum, they let the right to collect them to a tenant who was free to make what profit he could. At Stratford the college had in 1544 leased its tithes and other property for ninety-two years to William Barker, whose relative John sub-let them in 1580 to Sir John Hubaud. The situation then becomes extraordinarily confused; suffice it to say for our purposes that a lease of one half of the tithes of Old Stratford, Bishopton and Welcombe ended up in the hands of John's brother, Ralph Hubaud. This is what Shakespeare bought in 1605,[8] subject to annual payments of £17 to the Corporation (as the owners) and a further £5 to John Barker, the principal sub-tenant. A few years later[9] these tithes were actually valued at £60 a year, which would have left Shakespeare with an annual surplus in the region of £40. In ten years or so he would therefore have made good the £440 he had had to pay Hubaud; and for the remaining twenty-one years of the 1544 lease the £40 surplus would have been clear profit.

This succession of property deals, concluded within the space of ten years, is principally of interest against the general background of the time in demonstrating how Shakespeare's success in the theatre had enabled him to progress significantly in the social hierarchy. The son of a failing wool-dealer, he had established himself within twenty years as a 'gentleman', being described as such in his deeds and confirmed by the grant of arms to his father in 1596. Social mobility was very much a feature of the age: those who could make money had an excellent opportunity to invest it in the land that had come on to the market following the dissolution of the monasteries. Many of these new gentry were drawn from the ranks of lawyers, royal officials and merchants; others, previously yeomen, had managed to better their position through judicious land purchases. Shakespeare, on the other hand, as a playwright and theatre manager, had achieved entry into this élite band by an unusual route.

Before leaving the topic of Shakespeare's property, we must remember too that in 1601, on his father's death, he would have inherited the 'Birthplace' in Henley Street. Part of this became the home of his sister, Joan Hart, who in 1616 was listed as occupier in Shakespeare's will. The other, and larger, part was let to Lewis Hiccox and became an inn. This letting has recently been substantiated by an entry in the inventory taken on Hiccox's death in 1627, which refers to an unexpired term of years in a lease granted to him by William Shakespeare.[10] This in turn helps to explain two earlier references to Shakespeare's Birthplace in Henley Street which were discovered in 1864 in a bundle of deeds (now in the care of the Shakespeare Birthplace Trust) relating to the house next door. These describe the adjoining property, in 1609 and again in 1613, as the tenement 'late' of William Shakespeare.[11] That he had not sold it by then is clear, both from his will and other later evidence; but a long lease to Hiccox, almost certainly granted by 1606 and possibly by 1605,[12] is enough to explain why the word 'late' was used.

CHAPTER FIVE

The Highways Bill

New gentry in their midst could be of advantage to civic leaders if their good favour could be obtained. We have seen, even in the late 1590s, Sturley and Quiney discussing the advantage of persuading Shakespeare to invest in Corporation property. His attitude to an attempted enclosure at Welcombe, which we shall examine shortly, was also of vital interest to the Corporation and one on which it sought to influence him. His assistance was doubtless sought on other occasions, but we have only one known instance.

In the early years of the seventeenth century there was much concern about the state of the roads. Under the Highways Act of 1555 their maintenance had been made the responsibility of the parishes through which they passed, each parish being required to provide labour services to keep them in good order. This measure, however, proved quite inadequate and complaints about their condition multiplied. Three attempts were made in James I's first parliament to enact bills to remedy the situation. The first, introduced in February 1606, got no further than the committee stage before parliament was prorogued in May; the second, dealing only with Sussex, Surrey and Kent, and before the House in June 1607, failed because 'the bill was long and of much labour to the clerk' and, as no fees were forthcoming from those liable to benefit, the Speaker did not allow it to proceed;[1] and the third, introduced in March 1610, was also only at the committee stage when parliament was dissolved.[2] This did not put an end to good intentions: one Thomas Proctor published in 1610 *A profitable worke to this whole kingdom concerning the mending of all highways*, and in the same year the painter Nicholas Hilliard wrote to Robert, Earl of Salisbury, Principal Secretary of State, to recommend the suit of a labourer, William Goldsmith, who had discovered a new mode of repairing highways at half the usual cost.[3]

Such activity would have been of considerable interest to Stratford's leading citizens. An improvement in communications could do much to enhance a town's trading position and revive its flagging fortunes. In the early seventeenth century Stratford was bypassed by the principal trading routes. William Smith's *Particuler {sic} Description of England* (*c.* 1588) and William Harrison's *Historicall Description of Britaine* (1577) show no main roads to London nearer the town than those passing through Southam and Banbury, or through Evesham and Chipping Norton. Another gazetteer of 1603 shows no improvement in the situation.[4]

It is against this general background that we should consider a document in the Corporation records dated 11 September 1611, listing the names of seventy-one leading townsfolk.[5] It was intended, apparently, as a subscription list, for it is headed 'Collected towards the charge of prosecuting the bill in parliament for the better repair of the highways and amending divers defects in the statutes already made', and has against one name the sum of 2*s* 6*d*. No other document survives to illustrate its purpose, but it would seem clear that, following the failure of the three previous parliamentary bills (one of which can be directly attributed to lack of financial backing), a further attempt was being contemplated. A note of 19 February 1611 to the Earl of Salisbury speaks of letters being sent to local Justices of the Peace on the question of highway repairs and proposals survive, dating apparently from the autumn of 1611, for the repair of roads round London and afterwards throughout the whole of the country.[6] But parliament was not in session during this period, and indeed was not summoned again until April 1614. A new highways bill was almost immediately introduced, but again it failed as the king dissolved parliament in June before any Act had been passed.[7]

Our present interest in this list lies, of course, in its inclusion of the name of William Shakespeare. It was added, apparently, as an afterthought, or so we may infer from its being written in the right-hand margin, in contrast to the others, which form a column down the left of the page. Its position is not entirely arbitrary, however. The list begins with the names of the aldermen, bailiff and steward (all styled 'Masters') and continues with the names of two capital burgesses followed by Masters John Lane, John Combe, William Combe, Richard Tyler, John Nash and John Hall (Shakespeare's son-in-law), all styled in other documents 'gentlemen'. It is just above this group that Shakespeare's name occurs, corresponding with his rank in society (p. 47).

We cannot be sure why Shakespeare's name was originally left out, if indeed that is what happened. It is in the same hand and may in fact have been added almost immediately after the compiler realized his mistake. It has been suggested that the omission may have been due to Shakespeare's absence in London, even though this conflicts with another generally held belief that Shakespeare had retired to Stratford by 1611. This would not preclude, of course, the occasional visit to London, but it would seem odd for the compiler to have made the mistake he did if Shakespeare was by that time normally resident in Stratford. On the other hand, we might note that, although Shakespeare was certainly buried in Stratford in April 1616 and had been living at New Place when he first made his will a few months before, we cannot otherwise

The list of Stratford burgesses contributing to the expenses of a parliamentary bill for the better maintenance of the highways; 11 September 1611. Shakespeare's name was added on the right-hand side, as if as an afterthought. (SBT, BRU 15/1/4)

establish beyond doubt his presence in the town during this period; on the contrary, there is much to suggest that he was still involved in theatrical business.[8] If in 1611 Shakespeare was indeed more often in London than not, this would do much to explain the puzzling feature of this document.

Whether or not Shakespeare responded to the town's recollection that he might be able to help, we do not know. As mentioned above, only one receipt, that of *2s 6d*, is entered – against the name of the steward, Thomas Greene. Given the unfavourable political circumstances, the collection may never have been proceeded with.

CHAPTER SIX

Shakespeare and the Welcombe Enclosures

The last of the Stratford records to contain mention of Shakespeare (his burial apart) concern his involvement in the attempt to enclose a portion of the open fields in the manor of Old Stratford, Bishopton and Welcombe. The process began in 1614 and continued until well after his death two years later, and in the voluminous records relating to the story are seven references to the dramatist.

It would be difficult to identify a topic in Tudor England likely to arouse more passions than attempted enclosures. Often violence would flare, sometimes local but often regional, followed by commissions of enquiry, proclamations and parliamentary legislation aimed at combating the problem. Controversy was not the inevitable result of enclosure, but in areas of rising population and dwindling common land (one often the consequence of the other) resistance to enclosure was a reflex reaction of the local inhabitants. Folk memory reached back to the late fifteenth and early sixteenth centuries when many villages, including several in Warwickshire, had been completely depopulated as the result of enclosure. Warwickshire was also one of the counties affected by the great popular rising of 1549, fuelled primarily by agrarian unrest; and as recently as 1607 three thousand rebels had gathered at Hill Morton, in the north-east of the county, as part of a serious outbreak of rural violence on the Warwickshire/Leicestershire border, protesting against the 'incroaching tyrants [i.e. the enclosing landlords] who grind the faces of the poor'.[1] Rumours of an attempted enclosure at Stratford could therefore only be the cause of great concern; firstly, to the common folk who would suffer most; secondly, to those who would have to deal with, or feel the effects of, any outbreak of civil disorder; and thirdly, by some of the well-to-do (sometimes indistinguishable from those in the second group), who stood to lose financially if enclosure took place.

Why was enclosure such an emotive issue? Under the open-field system, a freehold estate might be made up of a number of small parcels scattered over a wide area. Enclosure involved an agreement between local freeholders to rearrange their holdings into compact blocks. In effect these became private estates which could be farmed independently, clearly to the advantage of the freeholder but not necessarily to the community at large. There was, for instance, a general fear that ancient common rights would be lost. Under the old system, stubble and harvest aftermath were surrendered to the whole of the village. Clearly this would come to an end on enclosure. Far more serious was the threat of depopulation that could follow from enclosure of arable land and its conversion to sheep pasture. Sheep husbandry required far less labour than arable farming and, not surprisingly, was almost universally associated in the popular imagination with unemployment, hardship and depopulation.

The government's response to this unrest was a series of investigations, culminating in legislation of 1563 that forbade further conversion to pasture and required a certain amount of retrospective restoration of arable land following recent enclosures. After thirty years of comparative calm this legislation was repealed in 1593. The timing could not have been more unfortunate: as we have seen, four disastrous harvests followed, reducing many to near starvation, and in 1597 the statute was re-imposed in order to preserve land for grain production.

A below-average harvest in 1607 and a bad one in 1608 coincided with outbreaks of violence in several Midland counties. In the enquiry that followed, nineteen Warwickshire parishes (including some, like Hampton Lucy and Salford Priors, close to Stratford-upon-Avon) were listed as having experienced recent enclosures.[2] Controversy, then, was assured when a few years later a partial enclosure of the common fields of Stratford was proposed. There was also an aggravating factor. In July 1614 a third serious fire in the town had brought further misery to the townsfolk. Enclosure, it seemed, was the final straw.

The official argument advanced by the Corporation against the scheme was a financial one. As one of the principal tithe owners it feared its income would drop, making it more difficult for it to discharge its functions under its charter. But one suspects there was more to it than this. Seven hundred of the population were alleged to be in receipt of poor relief and the fire in that year had caused general suffering. There was thus more than a possibility that a serious riot could break out as a result of this further provocation. No doubt many of the more well-to-do in the town sympathized with the poor in their misfortune, but mixed with this must have been a general fear for property if trouble broke out. As we shall see, the Corporation was later to be torn between opposing the enclosure and punishing those who took matters into their own hands.

In some respects the controversy is well documented, but in others tantalizingly imprecise. It is not easy, for instance, to identify the instigators of the scheme. The documents refer to Arthur Mainwaring of Shropshire and his agent, William

Replingham of Great Harborough, a relation by marriage. But as the dispute intensified these men disappear from the scene, and William Combe, one of Shakespeare's acquaintances and a prominent landowner in the area, emerges as the real villain of the piece. Although Mainwaring was alleged in various petitions to have recently bought land in Stratford, there is no other evidence of this. On the other hand Combe, at the very end of 1611, had bought a substantial freehold in the common fields from the lord of the manor of Stratford, and in the summer of 1614 had inherited from his uncle four enclosed fields in the neighbouring parish of Hampton Lucy.[3] The area selected for enclosure was at Welcombe, on the Stratford side of the parish boundary. It could well be, then, that the enclosure scheme was Combe's idea from the very start (part of a strategy to build up an estate of enclosed fields) and that Mainwaring, in the early stages, was just acting as his front man.

The first hint of trouble occurs in a document of 5 September 1614 when Thomas Greene, the town clerk, looked out a survey of the manor of Old Stratford made early in 1603, brought it up to date with his own annotations, and then appended to it a list of the current freeholders on the manor.[4] Shakespeare topped this list with the estate that he had bought from the Combes in 1602, with no one else holding more than about 15 acres. The purpose of the survey was to establish whose freeholds might be affected by the enclosure, as this could not be carried through without their owners' consent. If the Corporation could exert sufficient pressure on these key players, then the scheme could be thwarted. Shakespeare, according to Greene's note, held 'no common land nor ground beyond Gospel Bush', one of the limits, it was later said, of the proposed enclosure. It has been generally assumed, therefore, that Shakespeare's interests as a freeholder were not affected. Whether or not this was really so we will leave on one side for a moment; but it was also the case that

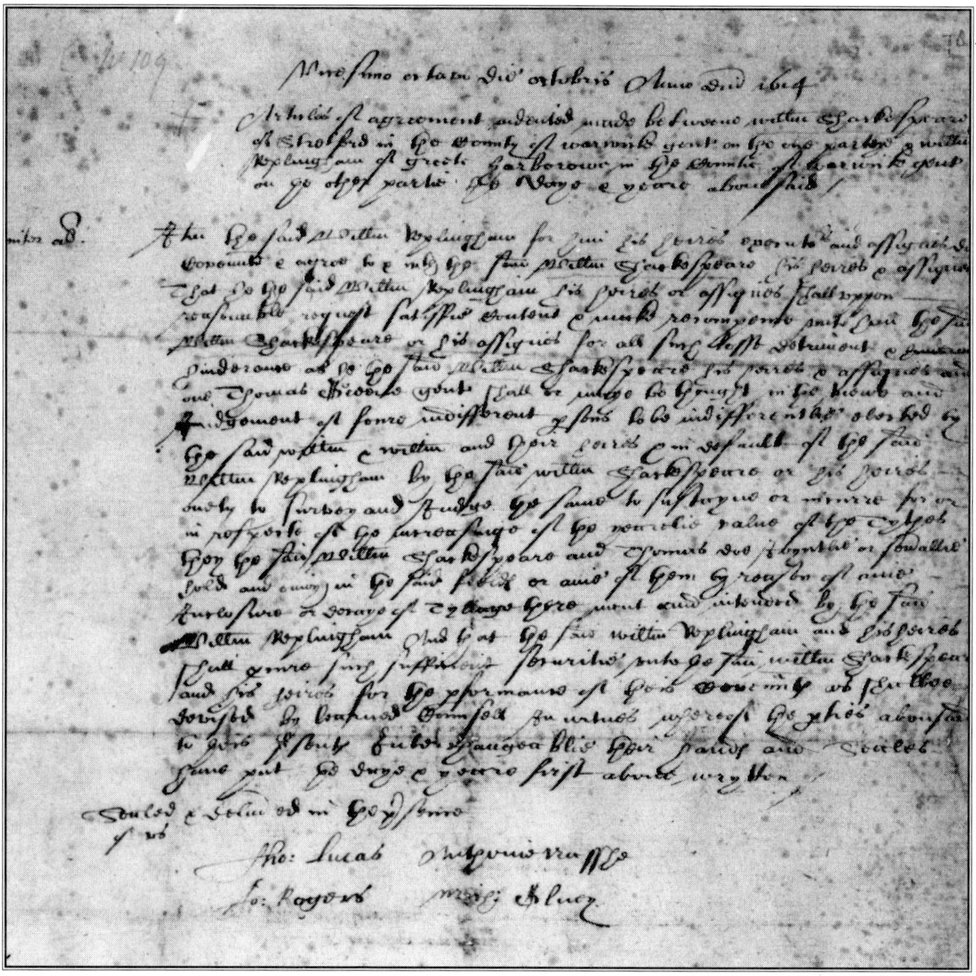

Contemporary copy of part of the agreement between William Shakespeare and William Replingham concerning the proposed enclosure at Welcombe; 28 October 1614. The marginal note, inter alia *('among other things') clearly shows that the copyist had only transcribed part of the original. (SBT, ER 27/3)*

Shakespeare, as one of the Corporation's tithe-tenants, stood to lose if his tithe-income should drop as the result of conversion of arable to pasture. The Corporation as owner of the tithes might therefore still have regarded him as a man worth having on their side. In this, however, it was to be disappointed. Shakespeare moved quickly and by 28 October had concluded an agreement with Replingham, recorded in the second of the enclosure documents that refer to the dramatist.[5] As it stands, this guaranteed Shakespeare against any losses that he might suffer 'by reason of any enclosure or decay of tillage', the losses to be estimated by 'four indifferent persons'. In other words, whatever Shakespeare may have felt on the matter of enclosures, he had not been averse to entering into discussions with the instigators of this particular venture in order to protect his financial interests; and although on this evidence alone it would be unfair to say he was in favour of it, he was clearly not passionately opposed.

But there is more to it than this. What we have before us today is not the original agreement but, as has long been recognized, only a near-contemporary copy. What has not been made clear, however, is that it is only a partial copy. Shakespeare and Replingham were not the only parties to the treaty. Thomas Greene, the town clerk, was also a tithe-tenant, and, according to his diary, which we will examine shortly, had had his name inserted into the agreement at the last moment. This diary and the copy agreement later found their way into the Corporation archives. Might it be, perhaps, that the copy was Greene's and that he had only bothered to have transcribed the clause which affected him and the Corporation, namely the one relating to the tithes? To show that this was almost certainly the case we have only to look closely at the copy. It begins with the date and a statement of the parties involved (but not mentioning Greene at this stage as he was only included as an afterthought). This is followed by the word

'*Item*' and the details of the arrangements to protect Shakespeare's tithe interests. Greene's name now appears, doubtless written in the original as an insertion, but now incorporated into the text. '*Item*' in this context means 'in like manner' and should have introduced not just this clause but others preceding it except the first which would have begun '*In primis*' ('in the first place'). In other words, these earlier clauses had been omitted by the copyist. We know this was so for in the left margin appear the words '*inter alia*' ('among other things') which was the customary manner of indicating omissions. What we have today, then, is a copy of only one clause, probably the last, and the only one affecting Greene's, and the Corporation's, interests, in whose papers it was later found (p. 53).[6]

What, then, did the other clauses contain? There is no certain answer to this, of course, but they may well have affected arrangements concerning those parts of Shakespeare's freehold property falling within the area proposed for enclosure. It has long been assumed, as we have seen, that there were no such lands. But we now have, to help us plot Shakespeare's estate, the recently discovered survey of his lands in the open fields.[7] Much work still needs to be done on identifying the precise location of the furlongs in which his scattered holdings were recorded, but even so there is good reason to suppose that some of them at least were liable to be affected by the enclosure. One of his parcels of land, for instance, containing 4 acres, was 'shooting and lying into Fords Green', a furlong which we know was to be partially enclosed.[8] He also had 'leas [areas of grassland] lying in the Dingles and about Welcombe Hills', other sensitive areas. It must surely have been the case that the missing clauses of the agreement dealt in some way with such land.

We should also remember that Shakespeare appears to have been on good terms with the Combe family. John Combe (the encloser's uncle and the member of the family principally concerned with the sale to Shakespeare of 107 acres in Old Stratford in 1602) left him £5 in his will, and Shakespeare himself bequeathed his sword (a very personal item) to Thomas (the encloser's brother) in the course of the dispute.[9] This was the man who on 26 December 1614 had called the members of the Corporation 'dogs and curs'.[10] Against such a background, it is not easy to cast Shakespeare in the role of a Corporation supporter.

The Corporation, however, mindful of public opinion, would enter into no deals and on several occasions reaffirmed in full council its opposition to the scheme. On 9 December members waited on William Combe to ask him to use his influence on their behalf. At this juncture Combe professed neutrality, but on 20 December came out into the open in support of Mainwaring (if indeed the scheme was not his own idea).[11]

From 15 October we are most fortunate in that the town clerk, Thomas Greene, kept a diary of the attempted enclosure so that we can follow the progress of the dispute in some detail; and it is this document that provides us with our other references to Shakespeare.[12] Greene, as we have just seen, was another of the Corporation tithe-tenants, and at the last moment had had his name inserted into Shakespeare's agreement with Replingham. This he recalled in his diary on 9 January 1615: 'Mr. Replingham articled with Mr. Shakespeare, and then I was put in.' But whatever his personal views he was also the council's executive officer, charged with the duty of resisting Combe's plans. In the second half of November he was in London to present a petition against the scheme, and on the 17th he records an interview with Shakespeare and his son-in-law, John Hall, on their 'coming yesterday to town'. Shakespeare showed himself remarkably well informed about the enclosure plans, detailing the area affected, stating that the land would be surveyed the following spring, but giving his opinion that 'there will be nothing done at all'. This again implies Shakespeare's less than neutral position, as does a further note Greene made on 10 December when, back in Stratford, he called at Shakespeare's home, New Place, in an unsuccessful attempt to see Replingham. Furthermore, following a council meeting on 23 December, at which further measures were agreed to halt the plans, Greene noted in his diary that he drafted letters both to Mainwaring and to Shakespeare 'with almost all the Company's hands [i.e. signatures of the members of the Corporation] to either', and sent a personal note to Shakespeare with 'copies of all our oaths made then, also a note of the inconveniences would grow by the Inclosure'. We have a copy of the appeal to Mainwaring pleading with him not to proceed, and entreating him to 'call to mind the manifold miseries this borough has sustained . . . wherein live above 700 poor which receive alms, whose curses and clamours will be daily poured out to God against the enterprisers of such a thing'.[13] We do not, regrettably, have a copy of the letters that went to Shakespeare and they could, of course, have been in an entirely different vein. But at the very least the Corporation must still have regarded him as a key player; otherwise they would not have contacted him at this stage.

As the Corporation feared, news of the enclosure plans inflamed popular opinion. The civic authorities then had to tread a delicate path between maintaining law and order (and punishing those who overstepped the mark) while continuing to oppose the scheme. Thus when the bolder spirits threatened direct action and declared their intention of filling in the enclosure ditches, Greene advised them to go as surreptitiously as possible 'so that none might see them go lest others might perhaps follow in company and so make a riot or a mutiny', congratulating himself later that 'I never gave the least allowance in any tumultuous courses but protested against it.' Violence did flare, however, and during a truce women and children from Bishopton boldly filled up the ditches that had been dug. After further threats, appeals and petitions to the local justices, the Corporation succeeded, on 2 April 1615, in obtaining an injunction against Combe's activities.

Combe did not give up, however, and the affair dragged on for several years. Shakespeare is mentioned on one further occasion in

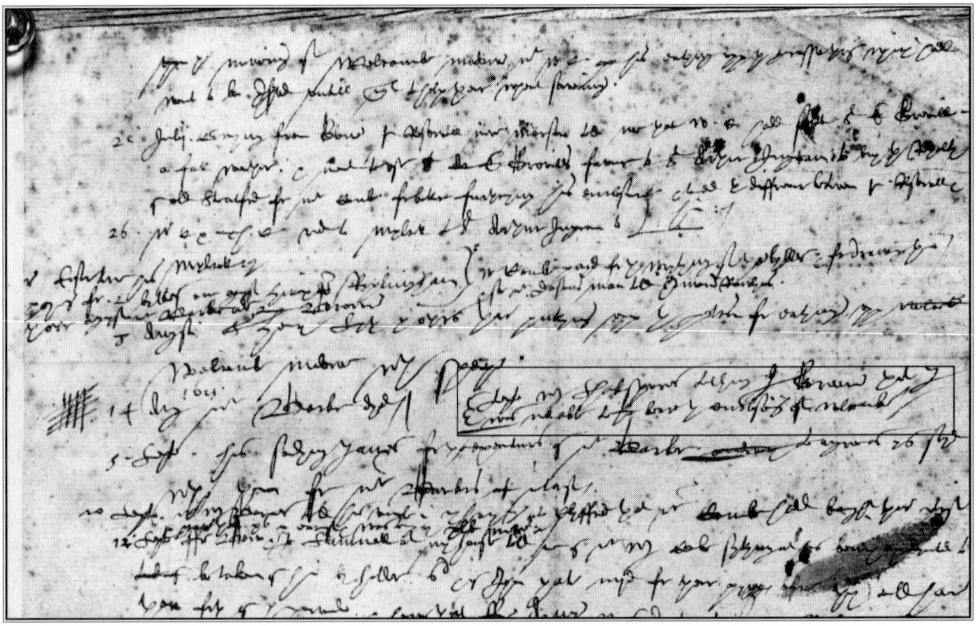

Extract from Thomas Greene's diary recording Shakespeare's comment on the proposed enclosure at Welcombe; September 1615. His hand is very difficult but within the highlighted entry can be seen a word beginning he . . . *crossed out and the word* beare *substituted for it. (SBT, BRU 15/13/29)*

Greene's diary, in September 1615. This is the most intriguing of all the entries for it hints at Shakespeare's own feelings: 'W. Shakespeare telling J. Greene [Thomas's brother] that I was not able to beare the enclosing of Welcombe.' Various attempts have been made to explain this passage, none of them entirely convincing. It has been suggested for instance that the passage beginning 'I was . . . ' represents direct speech and that it was thus Shakespeare who could not bear the enclosure. This is not very plausible, given what we know of Shakespeare's general attitude during the crisis, but the question then immediately arises as to why Thomas Greene should have bothered to record someone else's view of his own feelings. Greene, in fact, had started to write another word, beginning with the letters 'he', but had crossed it out and written 'beare' instead. Possibly, it has been suggested, he was going to write 'help' in the sense of 'prevent'; then, realizing the ambiguity of the word, intended to write 'bar' to make his meaning clear, but wrote 'beare' by mistake, thus confusing everybody (p. 58).[14] Had Shakespeare in fact expressed such an opinion (that opposition to the enclosure would not succeed), it would not be inconsistent with the overall impression that emerges from the documents that Shakespeare, far from being neutral (as is often claimed), had leanings towards the enclosure party.

CHAPTER SEVEN

The Documents: a Study in Survival

To many people it is a never-ending source of amazement that Shakespeare's life is apparently so poorly documented and that this most famous of all writers left behind him virtually nothing in his own handwriting. To archivists, however, this comes as no surprise; to them it would be asking too much to expect anything more.

Records survive, generally speaking, because they are part of a body of material looked after not by an individual, however much he or she may cherish them during his or her lifetime, but by some form of continuing institution. Parish registers and other church records are good examples, as are records of a local or national government body or those of a large landed family. Even these have suffered severe losses, but while their custody is vested not in an individual but a body of some permanence their chances of survival are much greater. An exception, of a sort, is title deeds. Before the days of registered title, purchasers took great care to ensure that all previous title deeds were handed over to them. These would then have to be passed on when the property was sold. No institution was providing custody here, but there were good reasons to make sure these items were not mislaid. Beyond this there was very little prospect, until recent times, of documentary material of a personal nature surviving for any length of time. In Shakespeare's case it is possible that some papers may have remained with his family until the death of his last direct descendant, Elizabeth Barnard, in 1670. But even this is by no means certain, and there is no reason after that date to expect them to have survived.

What we are left with, then, are passing references, mainly in official records. As far as Stratford is concerned most of these fall into three categories: entries in the parish register, the history of which we have already examined; the inclusion of Shakespeare's name in title deeds to his Stratford properties; and references to him in the Corporation of Stratford records. How these documents have come down to us, however, is far from straightforward.

Shakespeare's Title Deeds

The deeds recording Shakespeare's purchases of his Stratford properties would have been carefully guarded until such time as they were sold. These comprised the copy of the Rowington court roll, recording his acquisition of the Chapel Lane cottage; the deed (now lost) and fine for New Place; the conveyance (with its counterpart) of the 107 acres he bought from the Combes; and his lease of the Corporation tithes.

The subsequent history of the Chapel Lane document is the most straightforward and follows the history of the property. Under Shakespeare's will this copyhold estate passed to his daughter, Susanna, the wife of John Hall. Nothing further is heard until 1729, when it was held by Edward Clopton; as he by that time also owned New Place it seems likely that the small copyhold property nearby had descended with it, even though it is not mentioned in the intervening deeds concerning the estate. From 1729, however, its history is clear. It passed in 1755 to William Rawbone, in 1767 to John Butcher, and in 1770 to William Hunt, Stratford's town clerk. In 1848, when J.O. Halliwell published his

Life of Shakespeare, it was Hunt's grandson, W.O. Hunt, who held the title, and in whose possession Halliwell recorded the document testifying to Shakespeare's former interest in it. Clearly the deed had descended with the property. In 1864 Hunt presented it to the Shakespeare Birthplace Trust, where it has since remained.[1]

It was not Halliwell, however, who had discovered it. It bears in its top left-hand corner the letters 'E.M.' for Edmond Malone, and his reckoning of the date. This was the man, it will be remembered, to whom the vicar lent the parish register in 1788 when he was working on a new edition of Shakespeare's plays. Before April 1793 he had visited the town to conduct further research and then spent much of the summer of that year trawling through the Corporation records. In 1810 he recalled several visits, including a protracted one in 1794 (p. 63).[2] This must without doubt have been the period when the Chapel Lane document came to his notice. Its owner at that date would have been Charles Henry Hunt, who as town clerk would have known of Malone's examination of the Corporation archives. Indeed, he already knew of Malone's interest in matters Shakespearian, for in 1788, as the then owner of the site of New Place, he had been asked to look through his title deeds for any early material relevant to Malone's research.[3] Though nothing apparently came to light then we may assume it surfaced during further searches in the early 1790s.

Malone was unable to keep this discovery entirely to himself, for by 1821 the document had been seen and copied by a local antiquarian, Captain James Saunders.[4] William Hunt's son Thomas, who would have been the owner of it then, is elsewhere known to have helped Saunders in his antiquarian pursuits. Then, some twenty years later, W.O. Hunt brought it to the attention of two subsequent biographers of Shakespeare: Charles Knight, who mentioned it in his *William Shakespeare: a Biography* of 1843; and

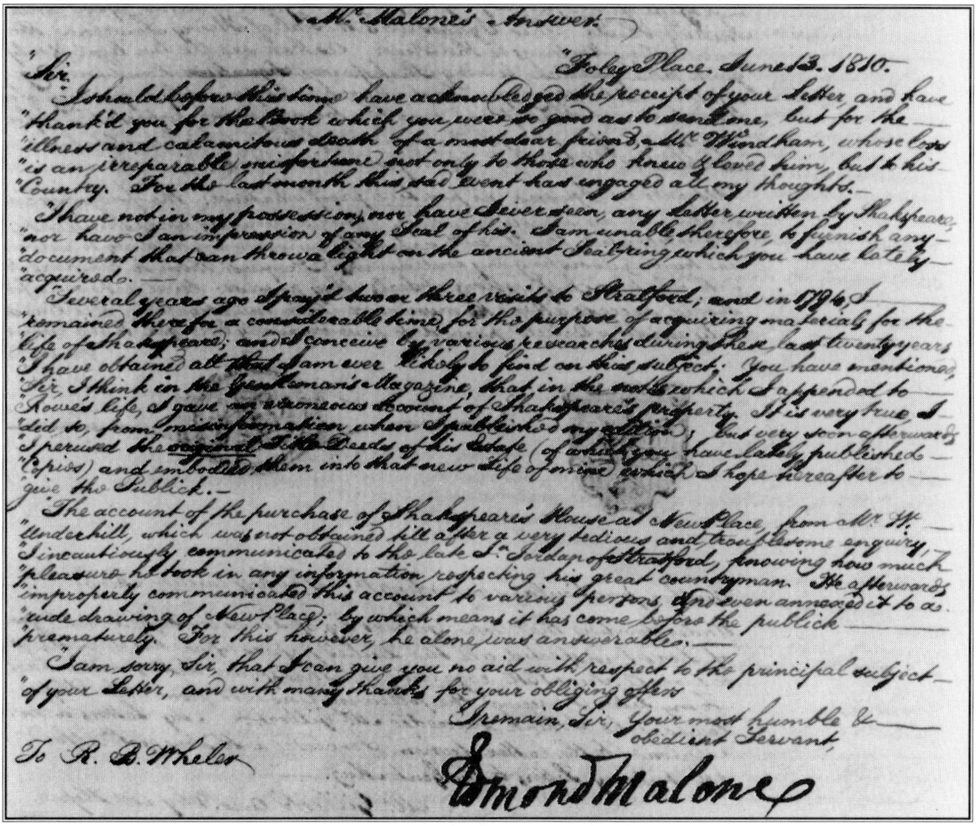

Mr. Malone's Answer.

"Sir. "Foley Place. June 13. 1810.

I should before this time have acknowledged the receipt of your Letter and have
"thank'd you for the Book which you were so good as to send me, but for the
"illness and calamitous death of a most dear friend, Mr. Windham, whose loss
"is an irreparable misfortune not only to those who knew & loved him, but to his
"Country. For the last month this sad event has engaged all my thoughts.—
"I have not in my possession, nor have I ever seen, any Letter written by Shakspeare,
"nor have I an impression of any Seal of his. I am unable, therefore, to furnish any
"document that can throw a light on the ancient Seal-ring which you have lately
"acquired.—
"Several years ago I pay'd two or three visits to Stratford; and in 1794, I
"remained there for a considerable time, for the purpose of acquiring materials for the
"Life of Shakspeare; and I conceive by various researches during these last twenty years
"I have obtained all ~~that~~ I am ever likely to find on this subject. You have mentioned,
"Sir, I think in the Gentleman's Magazine, that in the notes which I appended to
"Rowe's life, I gave an erroneous account of Shakspeare's property. It is very true I
"did so, from misinformation when I published my edition; but very soon afterwards
"I perused the original Title Deeds of his Estate (of which you have lately published
"copies) and embodied them into that new Life of mine which I hope hereafter to
"give the Publick.—
"The account of the purchase of Shakspeare's House at New Place, from Mr. W.
"Underhill, which was not obtained till after a very tedious and troublesome enquiry,
"I incautiously communicated to the late Mr. Jordan of Stratford, knowing how much
"pleasure he took in any information respecting his great countryman. He afterwards
"improperly communicated this account to various persons, and even annexed it to a
"rude drawing of New Place; by which means it has come before the publick
"prematurely. For this however, he alone was answerable.—
"I am sorry, Sir, that I can give you no aid with respect to the principal subject
"of your Letter, and with many thanks for your obliging offers
I remain, Sir, Your most humble &
obedient Servant,
To R. B. Wheler
Edmond Malone

R.B. Wheler's copy of Edmond Malone's letter to him; 13 June 1810. In this letter, Malone recalls his visit to Stratford in 1794 and particularly his perusal of 'the original title deeds' of Shakespeare's estate. (SBT, ER 1/8, p. 472)

James Orchard Halliwell, photographed in 1872. Many of the Shakespeare documents were printed for the first time in his Life of Shakespeare, *1848. (SBT)*

J. Payne Collier, who referred to it in the introduction to his edition of Shakespeare's works of 1844. It was J.O. Halliwell, however, in his *Life of Shakespeare* (1848), who first printed it in full.

The descent of the 1597 fine confirming the purchase of New Place, and the 1602 conveyance, with its counterpart, of 107 acres of land in Old Stratford is also fairly clear. These properties remained in Shakespeare's family until the death of his granddaughter, Elizabeth Barnard. They were then sold to Sir Edward Walker who willed them in 1677 to his only daughter, Barbara, wife of John Clopton of neighbouring Clopton House.[5] John was the local squire with a very considerable estate in and around the town. In 1702 he settled New Place and other properties on his second son, Hugh, as part of the arrangements made on his marriage;[6] but, being a family matter, there is no indication that any earlier deeds relating to these properties were sorted out and handed over. Indeed it is almost certain that they remained with the documents relating to the family's principal estate at Clopton, which eventually passed to the elder son. There they remained until the death of Frances Partheriche, the last of the Cloptons, in 1792.

It is fairly clear that during Mrs Partheriche's lifetime no proper examination of these papers was made: Malone had expressed an interest in them, but had been warned by the vicar that the owner was 'a very singular character and I am afraid by no means communicative'.[7] On her death, however, negotiations began for access to the material. The estate itself passed to distant relatives who spent most of their time in London, leaving the management of their newly acquired property to a local agent, Henry Wyatt. As early as May 1793 Wyatt had sent Malone an abstract of certain Clopton deeds and was being asked by Malone to arrange for originals to be sent to him in London.[8] This almost certainly occurred, for, writing in 1810, Malone recalled how in the early 1790s he had had the opportunity of perusing 'the *original* title deeds of his [Shakespeare's] estate'.[9] Again, however, he failed to publish his findings, and it was left to Stratford's first historian, Robert Bell Wheler, to announce in 1806 in his *History of Stratford* that Shakespeare purchased New Place in 1597 (which presumably he had learnt from an examination of the exemplification) and to give a complete transcript of the unexecuted counterpart of the Combe conveyance of 1602 and of three mid-seventeenth-century New Place title deeds. These he firmly stated were 'now in my possession'. Saunders also knew of these deeds for he actually transcribed the 1597 exemplification (p. 67), as well as the signed counterpart of the Combe conveyance, and copied out four further mid-seventeenth-century deeds relating to New Place, which in

Silhouette of Robert Bell Wheler (1785–1857), a Stratford solicitor and the author of the first history of the town. His and Captain James Saunders's notes contain the earliest copies of many of the Shakespeare documents (SBT)

1824 we know were in his house.[10] There can be little doubt, then, that the family agents, Henry Wyatt and his son Richard (who later took up residence at Clopton House and was accused of attempting to manipulate the estate in his favour),[11] had allowed the collection of family papers not only to be inspected by local enthusiasts but to have been plundered of some of its finest items. On Saunders's death those documents earlier recorded in his possession passed to Wheler and formed part of his collection, which was given to the Shakespeare Birthplace Trust in 1863 by his sister Anne. This also included the 1597 exemplification and the signed copy of the Combe conveyance of 1602. The unsigned counterpart is discussed below.

In confirmation of the fact that Wheler and Saunders did indeed acquire these items from the Clopton muniments we have only to consider the history of the deeds and documents that were left undisturbed. These surfaced early in 1886 as part of the collections of J.E. Severne, Esq., of Wallop, Hampshire, and were found to contain not only large numbers of Clopton papers but also some New Place title deeds that Wheler and Saunders had clearly missed.[12] Severne was the grandson of Anne, the adopted daughter and heiress of Mary Ingram of Little Wolford in Warwickshire. She

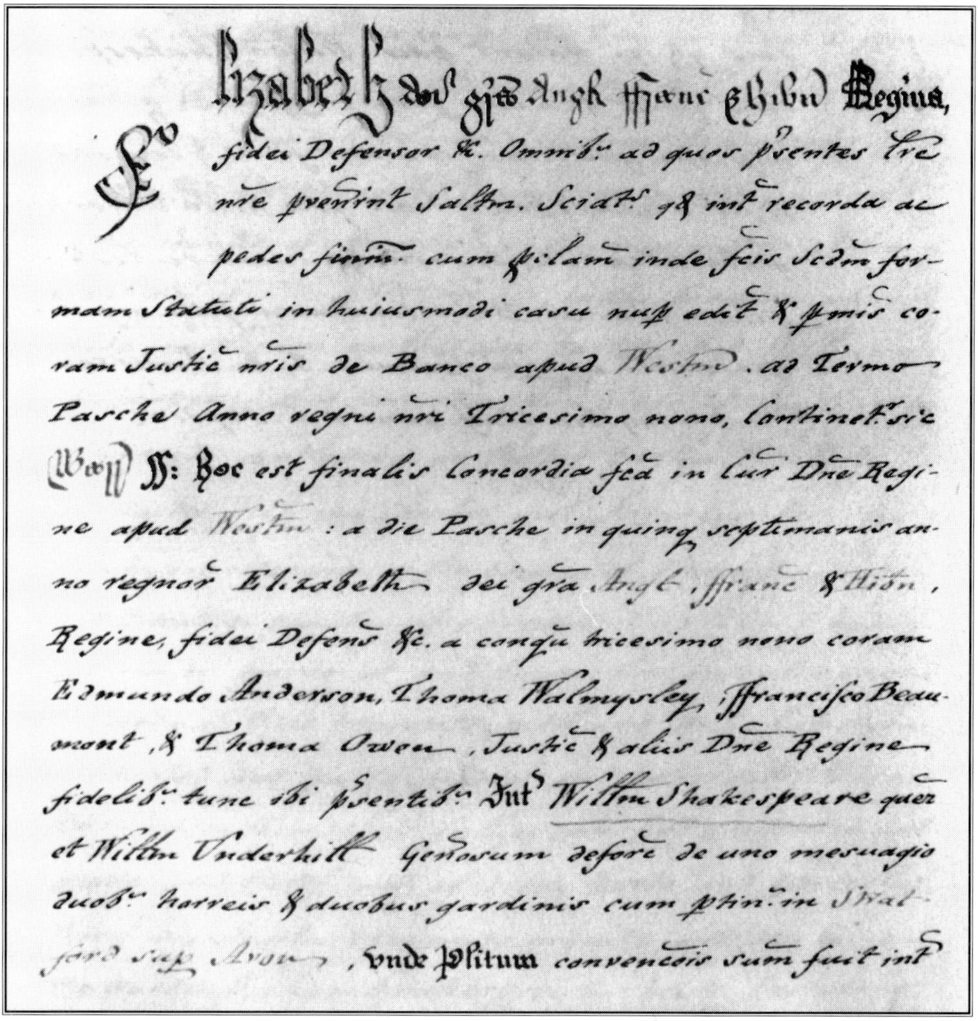

Elizabeth dei gra Angl ffranc et Hibn Regina,
fidei Defensor &c. Omnib3 ad quos p'sentes l're
n're pervenint Saltm. Sciat3 q'd int' recorda ac
pedes finiu cum p'clam inde fcis Scdm for-
mam Statuti in huiusmodi casu nup edit & p'mis co-
ram Justic n'ris de Banco apud Westm. ad Termo
Pasche Anno regni n'ri Tricesimo nono, Continet' sic
Warr ss: Hoc est finalis Concordia fca in Cur Dne Regi-
ne apud Westm: a die Pasche in quinq septimanis an-
no regnor Elizabeth dei gra Angl, ffranc & Hibn,
Regine, fidei Defens &c. a conqu tricesimo nono coram
Edmundo Anderson, Thoma Walmysley, ffrancisco Beau-
mont, & Thoma Owen, Justic & aliis Dne Regine
fidelib3 tunc ibi p'sentib3 Int' Willm Shakespeare quer
et Willm Underhill Generosum defore de uno mesuagio
duob3 horreis & duobus gardinis cum ptin' in Strat-
ford sup Avon, unde Plitum convencois sum fuit int'

Captain James Saunders's neat copy, c. 1820, *of the exemplification of the fine recording Shakespeare's purchase of New Place.* (SBT, ER 1/76, f. 54) in turn was the sister-in-law and heiress of the famous book and manuscript collector, Michäel Wodhull, and it was his collection (by that time owned by Severne) that formed the bulk of the items that were auctioned off in 1886.[13] It is a simple matter to explain how Wodhull came by these documents, for he was the executor of the will of Frances Partheriche, the last of the Cloptons of Clopton. She left her estate to Edward and John Ingram, distantly related to her, and less distantly to Wodhull's wife. The new owners, however, rarely visited Clopton, and at some point Wodhull, as executor, decided to remove the valuables. This is not mere speculation, for R.B. Wheler, writing in 1827 about a Van Dyck portrait that once hung in Clopton House, recorded that it was 'removed . . . to Wolford, near Shipston-on-Stour, the residence of the Ingram family, and from thence to Thenford where Michael Wodhull Esq. one of Mrs Partheriche's executors and trustees resided. Mr. Severne succeeded to Mr. Wodhull and in Mr. Severne's possession this picture . . . remains at Thenford.'[14] It can surely only be that the Clopton archives minus those removed by Wheler followed a similar course, thus becoming part of Wodhull's famous collection.

The unsigned counterpart of the Combe conveyance of 1602 has a slightly different history. This Wheler claimed was in his possession in 1805, and when Halliwell came to write his *Life of Shakespeare* in 1848 this was still the case. Yet it was not included in the 1863 gift to the Shakespeare Birthplace Trust of Wheler's papers. Quite what happened is not clear, but by 1930[15] it was known to be at Warwick Castle, and there it remained until 1972 when it was deposited at the Shakespeare Birthplace Trust by Lord Brooke. George Greville, Lord Brooke, and Earl of Warwick from 1853 to 1893, was well known for his interest in Shakespeare, and indeed had one of the rooms in the castle fitted out to house his

Shakespeare collection. It must therefore be assumed that he had been able by some means to secure possession of the Shakespeare document in question. A curious copy agreement survives in the Warwick Castle archives which may explain the process: by this the Earl of Warwick, in April 1864, agreed with J.O. Halliwell to pay to the latter's father-in-law, Sir Thomas Phillipps, an annuity of £240.[16] This was in return for Halliwell having granted to the earl a large collection of books, manuscripts and relics illustrative of the life and works of Shakespeare'. Could these have included the Combe document? If so, then Halliwell must, since 1848, have persuaded R.B. Wheler or his sister to part with it. On other occasions he is known to have been successful in such dealings. The New Place deeds still in the Severne collection in 1886, for instance, never reached the saleroom. They appeared instead the following year in the *Calendar of the Shakespearean Rarities . . .* preserved at Halliwell's home in Brighton. His acquisition of the Combe conveyance could be another example of just such opportunism. But whatever may have occurred, it is fitting that the two parts of this same transaction should once again have been brought together under the same roof.

Of Shakespeare's title deeds, it remains to consider the lease granted to him of a share in the Corporation tithes. His interest in these passed on his death to his daughter Susanna, the wife of John Hall. In 1625, however, the Halls surrendered this interest for £400 to the owners, the Stratford-upon-Avon Corporation, and, we may safely assume, their title deed to it.[17] This cannot be proved beyond all doubt as it was never actually recorded as being in the Corporation's possession. However, the many other surrendered leases in the Corporation's records clearly illustrate that handing them back was normal practice. Moreover, what does survive in the borough records to this day is the routine bond that Hubaud and

Shakespeare entered into when the lease was assigned, and which, we must assume, was also surrendered in 1625.[18] Here they lay, apparently undetected, until the summer of 1793 when Edmond Malone, the pioneer Shakespeare biographer, visited the town and, to use his words, by 'permission of the mayor, was allowed a complete rummage through all their papers'.[19] There is no real doubt that he discovered the document then, for in October of that year he wrote to the vicar of Stratford asking about Ralph Hubaud's family, for 'Shakespeare made a purchase from him, and among his papers, wherever they are, will indubitably be found some of the poet's letters'. [20] He also found in the Corporation's archives a draft of the 1605 assignment.[21] Originally this had not been dated, but in the margin Malone added an initialled note, '24 July 1605', establishing that he must have seen the original (p. 71).

This draft is of more than passing interest for, whereas the fair copying of legal instruments could safely be left to a clerk, the preparation of a draft would be the work of a trained lawyer, acting for either the vendor or purchaser. In the preparation of this draft some have detected the hand of the local lawyer, Francis Collins, who subsequently witnessed the fair copy and who is better known to posterity as a possible writer of Shakespeare's will.[22] In 1605 Collins would have been particularly well placed to have drafted Shakespeare's purchase of the tithes, for he was at that time a member of the Stratford Corporation, whose legal business he sometimes handled. Since the Corporation, as owner, had a legal interest in the tithes, Collins would have been able to look to their interests as well as Shakespeare's. Subsequently, we may assume, the draft remained in the Corporation archives among other working papers.

Malone never published the discovery of the transaction nor did it appear in his posthumous *Life of Shakespeare*. It was left to the Stratford antiquary R.B. Wheler to draw attention to its contents

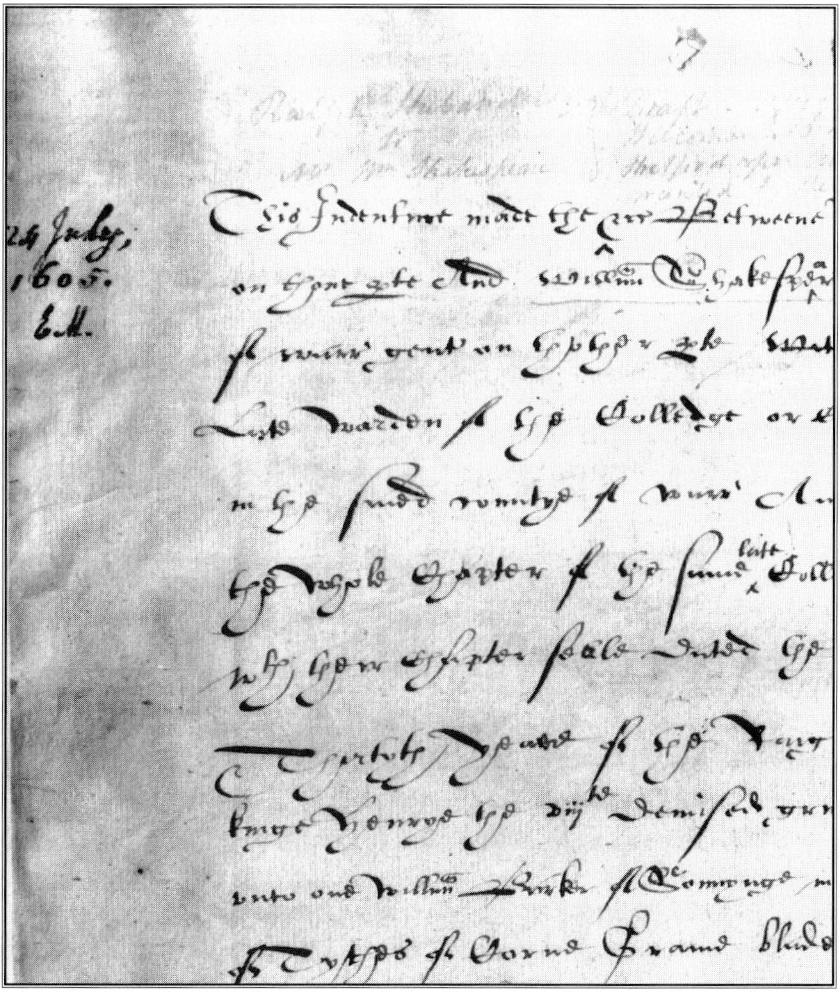
24 July,
1605.
E.M.

Edmond Malone's marginal note ('24 July, 1605. E.M.') added to the undated draft of Shakespeare's purchase of the Stratford tithes. He could only have known this after having discovered the original, probably in 1794. (SBT, BRU 15/2/2) in his *Guide to Stratford-upon-Avon*, which appeared in 1814. Around 1810 he and his fellow antiquarian, James Saunders (who was also a member of the Corporation), had begun a thorough investigation of the borough muniments, many of which were clearly 'borrowed' to copy at home. Some of these, like the deeds from Clopton, never found their way back to the muniment room and became instead part of Wheler's personal collection. Clearly the original Hubaud assignment was one of these; Saunders only saw (and copied out) the draft around 1821,[23] and even by the time J.O. Halliwell came to write his *Life of Shakespeare* in 1848 it was still only the draft of which he was aware. The original remained undetected in Wheler's papers until after his death in 1863, when the entire collection was presented by his sister, Anne Wheler, to the Shakespeare Birthplace Trust.

The Corporation Records

Like the Hubaud assignment, all the other documents we have considered were once, or still are, part of the Stratford Corporation muniments. These comprise the 'noate of corn and malt', the list of proposed contributors to the cost of the Highways Bill, the record of Shakespeare's court action against Philip Rogers, the four Quiney letters containing references to Shakespeare, Greene's diary, with its details of the attempted enclosure of Welcombe, and Shakespeare's agreement with Replingham made during the course of this same dispute.

Those with the least complicated history are the 'noate of corn and malt' and the Highways Bill subscription list. Both were known by 1821 to Saunders[24] and the first was subsequently printed by J. Payne Collier in his *Life of Shakespeare* of 1844. At that time the Corporation muniments were in the care of the town clerk and housed in the ancient Guildhall, but in 1862, following the restoration of Shakespeare's Birthplace, these records were moved to a specially furnished room there and since that date have been in the care of the Shakespeare Birthplace Trust. The Highways Bill subscription list remained unknown to the general public until Halliwell noted it in his 1848 *Life*.

Most of the other records have had a similar history, with the exception of a few items that, like the Hubaud tithe agreement, were removed by Wheler. The four Quiney letters, for instance, were kept by Quiney with other papers relating to his Corporation business in London. The last is dated December 1601, by which time he was serving as high bailiff. It is not surprising, then, that on his death (apparently the result of a brawl) the following spring they passed into the Corporation archives, and were bundled up and labelled 'a bundle of letters and diverse other matters concerning suits and petitions and other matters, concerning the Corporation . . . unsorted, bound up January 7 1603'.[25] There they remained until the summer of 1793 when some, if not all, were discovered during Edmond Malone's 'rummaging'. In September of that year he wrote to his friend, Thomas Percy, Bishop of Dromore: 'I have found a letter *to* him [i.e. Shakespeare] when in London, a very pretty little relick about three inches long by two broad [i.e. when folded]. His answer to this letter, the object of which was to borrow some money from him, would have been a great curiosity, and what is provoking is it ought to have been in the bundle where this was found (a parcel of letters to and from a Mr. Quiney whose son afterwards married the poet's daughter) and this should have been amongst the papers of Shakespeare's grand-daughter, wherever they are.'[26] Clearly it had not occurred to him that no reply from Shakespeare was found because Quiney's letter may never have been sent.

Malone did not otherwise advertise his discovery (except to tell another friend, Lord Charlemont, of it)[27] and it was left to Boswell to work it into Malone's posthumous *Life of Shakespeare*, published in 1821. Also featured in the appendix to this work was the letter of 4 November 1598 from Sturley to Quiney, so we need not really doubt that Malone had in fact discovered all four of the Shakespearian references. Certainly James Saunders saw them, for he copied all four on paper watermarked 1821.[28] But it was not until the 1840s that the remaining two letters were published. Charles Knight, who spent the summer of 1842 in Stratford researching, with Wheler's help, his life of Shakespeare, printed the letter of 24 January 1598 the following year. But it was not until J.O. Halliwell's *Life of Shakespeare* was published in 1848 that the undated note between the Quineys was first made public.[29]

Only three of these letters, however, are still in the Corporation muniments. The exception is the letter from Quiney to Shakespeare; indisputably part of the borough records when discovered by Malone in 1793, it was, at least by 1848 and probably for many years before, part of R.B. Wheler's papers. At what date he removed it is not known, but it is clearly yet another example of an item that drifted into his possession at a time when the real value of such material was not properly appreciated and the conditions under which it was kept far from secure. In the event it did not much matter, for, when R.B. Wheler's sister gave her late brother's collection to the Shakespeare Birthplace Trust, such 'borrowed' items came to rest alongside the collection of which they were once part.

This was also true of a page of Thomas Greene's diary concerning the Welcombe enclosures. The original manuscript comprised four sheets and, as Greene was town clerk, no doubt immediately became part of the Corporation muniments. One page was discovered by Wheler around 1810 and taken into his possession. From it he printed, in 1814, the Shakespearian entries of 17 November and 22 December. The other pages remained undetected in the Corporation papers until discovered by J.O. Halliwell sometime between 1848 and 1853. The 'note of freeholders' (including Shakespeare), also in Greene's hand, was known to James Saunders (who copied it out on paper watermarked 1821)[30] and was printed by J.P. Collier in 1844. It also formed part of the Corporation archives and was deposited at the Shakespeare Birthplace Trust with the rest of the collection in 1862. The first page of the diary, removed by Wheler and given to the Trust by his sister in 1863, has for convenience been reunited with the other pages.

The agreement between Shakespeare and Replingham, though again given to the Trust by R.B. Wheler's sister, was almost certainly another item removed by him from the Corporation records. This, as we have seen, was not Shakespeare's copy, but one made for Thomas Greene or the Corporation: indeed it is endorsed in a hand found in other Corporation documents relating to the enclosure.[31] It was copied by Saunders in or around 1821[32] and first printed, by Halliwell, in 1848.

Finally, the document recording Shakespeare's action against Philip Rogers, clearly once part of the Borough Court of Record's substantial archives, was also part of the Wheler bequest to the Trust in 1863. It had been copied by Saunders in 1821[33] and printed by Halliwell in 1848, and must also be reckoned as another of the items that Wheler removed from the Corporation records early in the century.

CHAPTER EIGHT

Conclusion

We must now summarize what these documents tell us, and in particular what, if anything, they reveal about Shakespeare the man. Certainly there is little, if anything, to remind us that we are studying the life of one who in his writings emerges as perhaps the most gifted of all time in describing the human condition. Here in Stratford he seems merely to have been a man of the world, buying up property, laying in ample stocks of barley and malt and, when others were starving, selling off his surpluses and pursuing debtors in court, and conniving, as it seems, at the Welcombe enclosures. We must firstly, however, guard against the assumption that Shakespeare oversaw every detail of his business affairs. Shakespeare, like anybody else who rather unexpectedly finds himself the possessor of wealth, would have looked round for someone to manage his affairs, especially while he was still actively involved in the London theatre. But who was his local man of business?

There are several possibilities, but the most likely is Anthony Nash. His father, Thomas, from Oxfordshire, seems to have worked his way into the gentry in the service of greater families. Anthony crops up frequently in Shakespeare's business dealings. He witnessed the Combe conveyance and Shakespeare's purchase of the Corporation's tithes. He managed the payment of Shakespeare's tithe rent to the Corporation[1] and also witnessed the Replingham agreement concerning the Welcombe enclosures. He was remembered in Shakespeare's will and his son later married the poet's granddaughter. No other local person can be shown linked with Shakespeare on so many occasions. Such a man may well have advised Shakespeare on sound investments, would have ensured at times of uncertainty that his house was well supplied with provisions, and would have been ready to advise Shakespeare on how best to protect his interests when the Welcombe enclosures were proposed.

This is not to suggest, though, that Shakespeare was a cypher and did not know what was going on. He had known what family hardship was when his father was faced with ruin. Through his own efforts he had more than recovered lost ground, advancing his family to the ranks of the gentry; in a town the size of Stratford his social equals were now few. He was not alone, of course, in his social achievement. Of the 230 or so gentry families in Warwickshire at the end of the seventeenth century, well over half had acquired that status since the 1550s.[2] But they were a select band, as a class jealous of their position and with a common interest to defend it. It would hardly have been possible for Shakespeare not to have been part of this system; and it is indeed the typical activities of a 'new' gentleman that these documents principally record.

Had Shakespeare's family not died out within two generations, further documentation on his life might well have survived. Even now it is still possible that more material could come to light. In the meantime we will have to make do with those precious few items which have come down to us. But, just as Shakespeare's plays are capable of different interpretations, so has the advance of scholarship enabled us to squeeze more out of the documents which record his life. This is because we no longer see them in isolation. They are part of an immense body of material that has enabled us over the years to build up a picture of urban life in

Shakespeare's day and of the social conditions of the time; and as we come to a greater understanding of these, so does Shakespeare's life take on a new dimension. He may have been the most gifted of all writers, but he was also inescapably a man of his time, preoccupied, like his contemporaries, with a multitude of problems and sharing with them their general attitudes and aspirations. Born into the ranks of the tradesmen who managed Stratford's affairs, he rose to the comparative heights of the much more select group of gentry whose good favour had to be sought. Whether or not this was a source of gratification to him we do not know, but as studies proliferate on the role and influence of this 'new' gentry so must we modify our view of some aspects of Shakespeare's life.

This survey has in part been carried out with this in mind. Although the number of Shakespearian documents in the Trust's care has remained more or less the same for many years, and although they have been examined and written about by countless scholars, recent contributions to our background knowledge of Elizabethan life make it possible to interpret them in a more informed way. We still do not know, of course (and probably never will), what Shakespeare's views were about the Welcombe enclosures or the civil unrest in Stratford caused by food shortages. Nor will we ever be sure about his personal feelings towards other Stratford townsfolk. But because thousands of similar documents have been used to piece together a wider knowledge of the background of Shakespeare's life, those few documents that mention him have in the process come to mean significantly more.

APPENDIX

The Shakespeare Documents at Stratford-upon-Avon

1. Parish register, Holy Trinity Church, Stratford-upon-Avon (DR 243/1)
   a) Baptism of William Shakespeare: 26 April 1564 (f. 5, baptisms)

   b) Baptism of Susanna, daughter of William Shakespeare: 26 May 1583 (f. 20v, baptisms)

   c) Baptism of Hamnet and Judith, children of William Shakespeare: 2 February 1585 (f. 22v, baptisms)

   d) Burial of Hamnet, son of William Shakespeare: 11 August 1596 (f. 29, burials)

   e) Burial of William Shakespeare: 25 April 1616 (f.46, burials)

2. Exemplification of the final concord recording the purchase of New Place by William Shakespeare from William Underhill: 4 May 1597 (ER 27/4a)

3. Letter from Abraham Sturley to Richard Quiney including mention that William Shakespeare was contemplating a purchase of land in Stratford: 24 January 1598 (BRU 15/1/135)

4. 'The noate of corn and malte' recording William Shakespeare as possessor of 10 quarters: 4 February 1598 (BRU 15/1/106)

5. Letter from Richard Quiney to William Shakespeare asking for help with a loan: 25 October 1598 (ER 27/4)

6. Letter from Adrian Quiney to Richard Quiney mentioning financial dealings with William Shakespeare: October 1598 (BRU 15/1/131)

7. Letter from Abraham Sturley to Richard Quiney making mention of William Shakespeare's assistance with a loan: 4 November 1598 (BRU 15/1/136)

8. Conveyance from William and John Combe to William Shakespeare of 107 acres in the common fields of Old Stratford: 1 May 1602 (ER 27/1)

9. Unsigned counterpart of the same transaction: 1 May 1602 (DR 232/1)

10. Copy of court roll of the manor of Rowington recording the assignment to William Shakespeare of a cottage in Chapel Lane, Stratford-upon-Avon: 28 September 1602 (ER 28/1)

11. Summons to Philip Rogers to appear at the Court of Record of the Borough of Stratford-upon-Avon in a plea of debt brought by William Shakespeare: 1604 (ER 27/5)

12. Assignment from Ralph Hubaud to William Shakespeare of a lease of part of the Stratford tithes: 24 July 1605 (ER 27/2)

13. Bond between the same parties for the performance of covenants: 24 July 1605 (BRU 15/2/3)

14. Draft of no. 12: [24 July 1605] (BRU 15/2/2)

15. Order by the Court of Record to arrest John Addenbrooke to answer to William Shakespeare on a plea of debt: 17 August 1608 (BRU 15/5/139)

16. Order to empanel a jury in the same case: 21 December 1608 (BRU 15/5/127a)

17. Names of the jury so empanelled: *c.* December 1608 (BRU 15/5/127b)

18. Order binding jurors to appear in the same case: 15 February 1609 (BRU 15/5/115)

19. Names of the jurors and their verdict in the same case: *c.* March 1609 (BRU 15/5/116)

20. Order to produce John Addenbrooke at the next court in the same case: 15 March 1609 (ER 27/6)

21. Order to produce Thomas Hornby as a surety for John Addenbrooke in the same case: 7 June 1609 (ER 27/7)

22. Conveyance of the property adjoining Shakespeare's Birthplace to the east, describing William Shakespeare's house as its neighbour: 20 July 160 (TTDI/83)

23. William Shakespeare listed as a contributor to a fund to promote a Highways Bill: 11 September 1611 (BRU 15/1/4)

24. Bill of complaint in a case in Chancery, Richard Lane and others (including William Shakespeare) v. Lord Carew and others, concerning the Stratford tithes: *c.* 1611 (BRU 15/2/11)

25. Survey of Corporation property recording William Shakespeare as a tithe-tenant: *c.* 1612 (BRT 2/1, p. 59)

26. Conveyance of the property adjoining Shakespeare's Birthplace to the east, describing William Shakespeare's house as its neighbour: 22 January 1613 (TTDI/85)

27. Thomas Greene's note of the ancient freeholders (including William Shakespeare) in the common fields of Old Stratford: 5 September 1614 (BRU 15/1/94)

28. Agreement between William Shakespeare and William Replingham concerning the Welcombe enclosure: 28 October 1614 (ER 27/3)

29. Thomas Greene's diary concerning the Welcombe enclosures, with four references to William Shakespeare's involvement: 1614–15 (BRU 15/13/26a–29)

30. Endorsement on lease of Clifford Charity land, showing William Shakespeare in possession of part of New Place Garden: 1603/1616 (ER 3/1979)

* * *

31. Payment by the Stratford Corporation to 'Mr. Shakespeare' for a load of stone [this could relate to Shakespeare's father, John, who did not die until 1601]: 1597–8 (BRU 4/1, p. 44)

Sources and Notes

Any investigation of the documentary sources for Shakespeare's life must rely to a great extent on two masterly works, *William Shakespeare, a Documentary Life*, OUP (1975), by S. Schoenbaum, and *William Shakespeare: a Study of Facts and Problems* (1930) by E.K. Chambers. References to these major sources have therefore been used sparingly on the assumption that the interested reader will either be familiar with them already or will wish to consult them as a matter of course. B. Roland Lewis, *The Shakespeare Documents* (1941), is also very useful, as is Mark Eccles, *Shakespeare in Warwickshire* (1961). Nobody has yet rivalled Edgar Fripp for a knowledge of the Stratford background to Shakespeare's life, but his books need to be read in conjunction with more recent work on the period. For the Shakespeare documents lodged at the Public Record Office, see D. Thomas, *Shakespeare in the Public Records*, HMSO (1985).

Introduction

1. D. Thomas, *Shakespeare in the Public Records*, HMSO (1985).

Chapter One

1. Appendix, no. 1.
2. M. Ingram, *Church courts, sex and marriage in England, 1570–1640* (1987), pp. 219–21.
3. For another six there is no evidence either way.
4. See E.A. Wrigley and R.S. Schofield, *The population history of England* (1981), p. 255. J.M. Martin, however, suggests a lower age for men at marriage in Stratford during the 1570s and 1580s ('A Warwickshire market town in adversity: Stratford-upon-Avon in the sixteenth and seventeenth centuries', *Midland History*, vii (1982), p. 28), as does Jeanne Jones, but on the evidence of a limited sample ('A community study of sixteenth century Stratford-upon-Avon', unpublished M. Phil., University of Birmingham, 1991, p. 84).
5. J.T. Murray, *English dramatic companies, 1558–1642* (1910), i, p. 94.
6. See especially S. Porter, 'From death to burial in seventeenth-century England', *Local Historian*, vol. 23, no. 4 (Nov. 1993), pp. 199–204.

7. *The Vestry minute-book of the parish of Stratford-on-Avon from 1617 to 1699 A.D.* (1899), pp. 5–6.

8. The original notes sent to Garrick have only recently come to light, and were sold at Phillips in London on 19 March 1992 (see its catalogue of that day *Autograph letters, manuscripts, books, atlases and maps*, Lot 26). Their discovery requires minor modification to S. Schoenbaum's comments in *William Shakespeare: a documentary life* (1975), p. 23.

9. E. Malone, *The correspondence of Edmond Malone . . . with the Rev. James Davenport DD, vicar of Stratford-on-Avon* (1864), *passim*. Some of Davenport's draft replies are preserved at the Shakespeare Birthplace Trust [SBT] (ER 88) and a few originals survive in the Bodleian Library (MS. Eng. letters C 15).

10. G. Arbuthnot, *Two hours in Stratford-on-Avon; an itinerarium* (1889), p. 24; and see, for example, R.G. White, *England without and within* (1882), pp. 520–1.

Chapter Two

1. He paid £320 for the 120 acres in Old Stratford and £440 for the tithes. The purchase price of New Place is not known, but would have been in the region of £150. For wage rates, see J. Thirsk (ed.), *The Agrarian History of England and Wales*, iv (1967), p. 864, where the daily wage rate for agricultural labourers during this period is given as 8*d*.

2. Appendix, no. 2.

3. Thomas, *Shakespeare in the Public Records*, pp. 21–2.

4. For local examples, see SBT, DR 10/803, 819, 1214, where another 'new man', Arthur Gregory, a Coventry lawyer, had his purchase of local manors recorded in this way.

5. Folger Shakespeare Library, Zc 36/100, 103.

6. SBT, BRT 1/2/533.

7. J.O. Halliwell, *An historical account of the New Place, Stratford-upon-Avon* (1864), pp. 212–14.

8. Appendix, no. 30.

9. Folger Shakespeare Library, Zc 36/100.

10. Halliwell, *New Place*, pp. 13–15.

11. *Minutes and accounts of the Corporation of Stratford-upon-Avon, 1586–92*, Dugdale Society, x (1929), p. 106.

Chapter Three

1. On this topic generally see Martin, 'A Warwickshire market town in adversity'; S. Porter, 'Fires in Stratford-upon-Avon in the sixteenth and seventeenth centuries', *Warwickshire History*, iii, no. 3 (Summer 1976), pp. 97–105;

A. Dyer, 'Warwickshire towns under the Tudors and Stuarts', ibid., iii, no. 4 (Winter 1976/7), pp. 122–35.

2. For threatened risings in Oxfordshire, Norfolk and the West Country, see *Calendar of State Papers, Domestic, 1595–7*, pp. 316–20, 323, 325, 342–5, 401, and for other disturbances in Wiltshire, Oxford, Kent, London and Sussex, A.B. Appleby, *Famine in Tudor and Stuart England* (1978), p. 142.

3. SBT, BRU 15/2/18.

4. E.I. Fripp, in *Master Richard Quyney* (1924), collects together the relevant facts but subjects them to no analysis.

5. Appendix, no. 3.

6. Warwickshire County Record Office, CR 1886/BB711/2663. This is printed in part in *Minutes and accounts of the Corporation of Stratford-upon-Avon, 1593–1598* (Dugdale Society, xxxv, 1990), pp. 48–50, but by a strange omission only eight households are listed, whereas the original covers over a hundred. A quarter in this context was a measure of capacity (traditionally 8 bushels), not a measure of weight.

7. For tables showing the quality of English harvests and the price of wheat see *Agricultural History Review*, xii (1964), p. 39 and facing p. 29.

8. In 1597 the number of burials (*c.* 180) was the highest since the serious plague outbreak of 1564, and was not exceeded again throughout the seventeenth century.

9. *Acts of the Privy Council*, xxvii, p. 359. See also Historical Manuscripts Commission [HMC], *Calendar of the manuscripts of the Marquis of Salisbury*, vii, pp. 296, 410, 497, 526.

10. Appendix, no. 4. Printed in full, *Minutes and accounts, 1593–1598*, pp. 135–40.

11. SBT, BRU 15/1/140.

12. Appendix, no. 11.

13. Appendix, nos 15–21.

14. S. Schoenbaum, *William Shakespeare: a compact documentary life* (1977), pp. 240–1.

15. *Minutes and accounts, 1593–1598*, pp. 134–5.

16. SBT, ER 1/97, f. 127; BRU 15/1/140.

17. *Minutes and accounts, 1593–1598*, pp. 73, 86–7; BRU 15/12/48.

18. SBT, ER 1/97, pp. 127–127v.

19. SBT, BRU 15/1/140.

20. SBT, BRU 15/1/135.

21. Ibid.

22. SBT, ER 1/97, f. 134.

23. Appendix, no. 5.

24. Appendix, no. 7.

25. Halliwell, *Life of William Shakespeare* (1848), pp. 12–13; E.A.J. Honigmann, '"There is a world elsewhere"; William Shakespeare, businessman', in W. Habicht and others (eds), *Images of Shakespeare* (1988), pp. 40–6.

26. Appendix, no. 6.
27. SBT, BRU 15/1/124.

Chapter Four

1. Appendix, no. 10.
2. B.R. Lewis, *The Shakespeare documents* (1941), ii, p. 352.
3. Appendix, nos 8 and 9.
4. Chambers, *William Shakespeare*, ii, p. 110.
5. SBT, DR 37/Box 113/15. See M. Macdonald, 'New discovery about Shakespeare's estate in Old Stratford', *Shakespeare Quarterly* (xlv, no. 1, Spring 1994).
6. Her children were baptized and buried in Stratford during the years 1616–38.
7. See Schoenbaum, *William Shakespeare*, pp. 240–1.
8. Appendix, no. 12.
9. *c.* 1611, when Shakespeare was named as an interested party in a Chancery case concerning the Stratford tithes (Appendix, no. 24).
10. Hiccox's inventory is now in the Hereford and Worcester County Record Office: the entry was discovered by Jeanne Jones in 1992.
11. Below, Appendix, nos 22 and 26. In fact the word *late* has been inserted in the 1609 deed, possibly in the hand of the writer of the 1613 one. See also J.O. Halliwell, *Abstracts and copies of indentures respecting estates in Henley Street . . .* (1866), where there is an account of how the deeds were discovered.
12. That is, the dates of surviving grants to Hiccox of an innkeeper's licence, in the later case for a tavern stated to be in Henley Street: SBT, BRU 15/3/23, BRU 15/12/75.

Chapter Five

1. *Journal of the House of Commons*, i, pp. 262, 264, 381, 387–8.
2. Ibid., pp. 408, 415–16, 427.
3. *Calendar of State Papers, Domestic, 1603–1610*, p. 595.
4. *English Historical Review*, xxxiii (1918), pp. 234–43.
5. Appendix, no. 23.
6. *Calendar of State Papers, Domestic, 1611–1618*, pp. 10, 91.
7. *Journal of the House of Commons*, i, pp. 465, 476.
8. The evidence is cited in Schoenbaum, *William Shakespeare*, chapter 14, although the author still appears to favour the idea of an earlier retirement.

Chapter Six

1. For early enclosure in Warwickshire, see W.E. Tate, 'Enclosure Acts and awards relating to Warwickshire', *Trans. Birm. Arch. Soc.*, lxv (1943–4), pp. 45–104.
2. Ibid. An apparent attempt by Stratford's lord of the manor to enclose common land within the town in 1601 was also stoutly resisted (Fripp, *Master Richard Quyny*, pp. 170–82).
3. SBT, ER 3/321; Halliwell, *Life of William Shakespeare*, p. 235.
4. Appendix, no. 27.
5. Appendix, no. 28.
6. For the subsequent history of the copy agreement, see below, p. 75.
7. Above, pp. 40–1.
8. C.M. Ingleby, *Shakespeare and the enclosure of common fields at Welcombe* (1885), p. xii.
9. Thomas, *Shakespeare in the Public Records*, pp. 23, 27.
10. According to Greene's diary: see Appendix, no. 27.
11. Ibid.
12. Appendix, no. 29. The entire document is transcribed in C.M. Ingleby, op. cit.
13. SBT, ER 1/1/66.
14. M. Eccles, *Shakespeare in Warwickshire* (1961), p. 138.

Chapter Seven

1. In 1899 Hunt's son Thomas presented the other deeds recording the property's later history (SBT, ER 3/475, 477–9).
2. SBT, ER 1/8, p. 472.
3. Malone, *Correspondence . . . with James Davenport*, p. 13.
4. SBT, ER 1/76, f. 120v.
5. SBT, TTD II, no. 21.
6. Ibid., nos 24–6.
7. Bodl., MS Eng. letters C 15, ff. 46–7.
8. Malone, *Correspondence . . . with James Davenport*, pp. 71–2.
9. SBT, ER 1/8, p. 472.
10. SBT, ER 1/76, ff. 54–64v, 66–69v, 72–73v.
11. SBT, DR 52/11.,
12. *Athenaeum*, 13 February 1886 (p. 241); 20 March 1886 (p. 401).
13. For a copy of the relevant Sotheby's catalogue see SBT, DR 286/24.
14. SBT, ER 1/8, p. 183.
15. E.M. Greville, *Warwick Castle* (1938), p. 58.
16. Warwickshire County Record Office, CR 1886, Box 789/61.

17. SBT, BRU 8/17/18.
18. Appendix, no. 13.
19. So he wrote to his friend, James Lord Charlemont (HMC, *Manuscripts of the Earl of Charlemont*, ii, pp. 220–1).
20. Malone, *Correspondence . . . with James Davenport*, p. 81.
21. Appendix, no. 14.
22. See, for instance, Eccles, *Shakespeare in Warwickshire*, p. 141; Chambers, *William Shakespeare*, ii, p. 174.
23. SBT, ER 1/76, f. 119v. The draft was later lent to J.P. Collier: see his 'Life of William Shakespeare' (p. ccxii) published in 1844 in vol. 1 of his edition of Shakespeare's works.
24. Ibid., ff. 92–5, 99–100.
25. SBT, BRU 15/1/137.
26. Bodl., Malone Ms. 26, ff. 21–2.
27. HMC, *Charlemont*, ii, pp. 220–1.
28. SBT, ER 1/76, ff. 75, 77v, 80–1, 122.
29. Halliwell, *Life of William Shakespeare*, p. 175.
30. SBT, ER 1/76, f. 98v.
31. For example, SBT, BRU 15/7/5, 7.
32. SBT, ER 1/76, f. 95v.
33. Ibid., f. 74.

Chapter Eight

1. Halliwell, *Life of William Shakespeare*, pp. 103, 105.
2. A. Hughes, *Politics, Society and Civil War in Warwickshire* (1987), p. 29.

Index